D1329936

NABOKOV
The Dimensions of Parody

DAVID GLENN HUNT
MEMORIAL LIBRARY
GALVESTON COLLEGE

NABOKOV
The Dimensions of Parody

DABNEY STUART

Louisiana State University Press
BATON ROUGE AND LONDON

DAVID GLENN HUNT
MEMORIAL LIBRARY
GALVESTON COLLEGE

Copyright © 1978 by Louisiana State University Press
All rights reserved
Manufactured in the United States of America

Designer: Dwight Agner
Type face: VIP Electra
Typesetter: The Composing Room of Michigan, Inc.
Printer and binder: Kingsport Press, Inc.

LIBRARY OF CONGRESS CATALOGING IN PUBLICATION DATA

Stuart, Dabney, 1937–
  Nabokov: the dimensions of parody.

  1. Nabokov, Vladimir Vladimirovitch, 1899–1977
Criticism and interpretation. I. Title
PG3476.N3Z89   813′.5′4   77–20870
ISBN 0–8071–0384–5

Contents

CONTENTS

Abbreviations

I have used the following abbreviations to simplify the procedures of reference to Nabokov's works:

BS *Bend Sinister*
D   *Despair*
G   *The Gift*
IB *Invitation to a Beheading*
LD *Laughter in the Dark*
LH *Look at the Harlequins*
P   *Pnin*
SK *The Real Life of Sebastian Knight*
SM *Speak, Memory: An Autobiography Revisited*
SO *Strong Opinions*

Preface

Despite the truth of Mikhail Lermontov's statement that "readers are generally not concerned with moral purposes or with attacks in reviews, and in result, do not read prefaces," I have always been an avid reader of them, and now believe it in the interest of this little book that I write one. A volume of literary criticism always causes expectations to rise for the reader, as, under particular circumstances, quills come to attention on the back of a porcupine. Certain of those expectations will, I suspect, not be met by these chapters, and an alert may spare the reader irrelevant disappointments.

To begin with, insofar as I advance a thesis it is modular, as the chapter titles indicate. I do deal with certain recurrent thematic and perceptual matters, but I do not seek an overriding theoretical coherence under which those concerns may be subsumed. These are "readings in" certain books by Nabokov, not an exhaustive study of his works.

Secondly, the books with which Nabokov is most widely and immediately identified—*Lolita, Pale Fire,* and *Ada*—I do not confront, except by occasional allusion. When I began the first of these essays some years ago one of the conscious choices I made was to write about the shorter, less remarked novels. Although it might seem a better book to place under my heading "the novel as game," I have also omitted *The Defense*, for two reasons: my knowledge of chess is insufficient to the task, and my use of the term "game" (as I hope my comments on *Sebastian Knight* show) refers more to the modality and tone of the novel, *qua* novel, than to the use of a particular game (like chess) as a structural guide. *The Defense* is a tour de force in this context; *Sebastian Knight* is a paradigm.

These are negative cautions, and while a reader might accept the focus on the shorter novels, he might justly ask what *does* constitute the coherence of the volume if the author eschews the usual theoretical predispositions that control such studies? I have attempted two compositional strategems. The more obvious I have mentioned; it is suggested by the title of the book, and by its chapter titles and subheadings: certain of Nabokov's novels considered as modally something other than novels, and then (after a mild foray into a thematic refusal, not altogether a tangent) his own autobiography seen as fiction. I envision the book from this perspective as a circle, around whose edges one travels while looking toward its center; or as a rotating prism with a stationary audience. In less graphic terms, it is possible to consider these approaches as specifications of parody.

And I have tried, secondly, to make the progression of the book mirror a movement from the appearance of informative commentary to the appearance of possible fiction. Thus the last three chapters (perhaps beginning earlier, with the "Udo Conrad" section of Chapter Four) are less embroiled with detailed discussion (though no less dependent on detail) than are the first four. A shift occurs in my chapter on *Pnin* after I have considered the novel as biography. I intend the rest of that chapter to mimic more than comment, and certain devices (the address to the reader, and its counterpoint, for example) in the final chapter signal a conscious veering toward parody itself, seen as subject matter earlier, but used, or almost used, as a mode of composition in the end. My aim, inadequately adumbrated here, is to have my book assumed by its subject, and the reader, a companion in these divagations, returned there, too.

Acknowledgments

Modern Language Quarterly: Parts of the first and second chapters were excerpted and rearranged, and appeared here under the title now affixed to Chapter Two, "Angles of Perception" (XXIX [September, 1968], 312–28). Similarly, parts of Chapter Seven were deleted, and the rest altered and compressed, and appeared under the title "The Novelist's Composure: *Speak, Memory* as Fiction" (XXXVI [June, 1975], 177–92).

University of Windsor Review: Since "All the Mind's a Stage" appeared here (IV [Spring, 1969], 1–24) I have substantially revised its explicit theoretical base.

Tri-Quarterly: Chapter Four appeared here as "*Laughter in the Dark*: The Dimensions of Parody" (XVII [Winter, 1970], 72–95). In response to Nabokov's comments on the essay as it appeared in *Tri-Quarterly* I have added some dimension to the section involving doubles.

Georgia Review: Chapter Five was printed here (XXX [Summer, 1976], 432–46) with what were called "minor" alterations in diction. I consider them more important, however, and the reinstatement in this book of certain words and phrases allows a denser echoing of the novel. I have also restored the notational matter (deleted, or incorporated into the text in the journal version) and have in general increased such material throughout the volume.

ACKNOWLEDGMENTS

Makers of the Twentieth Century Novel, edited by Harry Garvin (Lewisburg, Pa.: Bucknell University Press, 1977): Chapter Six initially appeared in this volume under the title *"Pnin*: Floating and Singing."

In each of the above cases I am grateful for permission to reprint material that has previously appeared.

Acknowledgment is made also for permission to quote from the following books by Nabokov: to New Directions Publishing Corporation for *The Real Life of Sebastian Knight*, 1941, © 1959 by New Directions, and for *Laughter in the Dark*, © 1938 by Vladimir Nabokov; to G. P. Putnam's Sons for *Invitation to a Beheading*, © 1959, *Despair*, © 1966, and *Speak, Memory*, © 1966; and to Doubleday and Co. for *Pnin*, © 1957.

Usually over long distances, the following people made suggestions about the composition of this book, which, I like to think, caused improvements of a kind too complicated and delicate to trace. I wish to thank them for their help: Edith Baras, Richard Johnson, Harry Garvin, Roger Sale, William Matchett, David Wagoner, and Julian Moynahan. In the manual preparation of the manuscript the help of Jeannette Jarvis, Sandra Vinson, and Beverly Jarrett was invaluable.

I am particularly indebted to Washington and Lee University, which gave me both a summer grant and a term's leave, without which I would have been a longer decade than I was finishing the work.

NABOKOV
The Dimensions of Parody

ONE

The Real Life of
Sebastian Knight:
An Introduction
to Central Modes

I THE NOVEL AS GAME

In the preface to his English rendition (1965) of *The Eye* (1930) Vladimir Nabokov writes, "The texture of [this] tale mimics that of detective fiction but actually the author disclaims all intention to trick, puzzle, fool, or otherwise deceive the reader." Later on in the same context he continues, "I do not know if the keen pleasure I derived 35 years ago from adjusting in a certain mysterious pattern the various phases of the narrator's quest will be shared by modern readers, but in any case the stress is not on the mystery but on the pattern."[1]

The narrator of *The Real Life of Sebastian Knight* characterizes Sebastian Knight's first novel, *The Prismatic Bezel*, as "a rollicking parody of the setting of a detective tale" filled with "obscure fun," although the narrator, Sebastian's half brother, tells us in the same breath that the parody and fun are springboards for the author to leap to other, quite different

1. *The Eye* (New York: Phaedra, 1965).

1

concerns.[2] I think this commentary on Sebastian's first book is intended to be as well a commentary on the biography of Sebastian his half brother is writing. Both Nabokov and Knight parody detective fiction, and it's a small move from the specific parody to the general consideration of the novel itself as a form of detection, a game of obscure fun, a mysterious composition in which the stress is on the pattern. I will be aiming my discussion at what the parody is the springboard for, since Nabokov also uses the novel-as-game to lead his readers to an understanding of the novel as something more. Nonetheless, it remains a game.

The general structure of *The Prismatic Bezel* ("bezel" usually refers to the multifaceted surface of a cut jewel) mirrors the general structure of *The Real Life of Sebastian Knight*. In *Bezel* a man called G. Abeson is murdered, and the initial chapters of the book concern the search for the killer. This takes some time, however, since the investigating detective is waylaid and is very late arriving at the boarding house where the killing occurred. During this time it is gradually revealed that everybody in the boarding house is related somehow, and the boarding house becomes a country house. As this happens the style of the book changes so that the reader forgets the mystery, and begins to think he is in the surroundings of friendly, social experience. When the tardy inspector appears, the whole novel is thrown back into its opening atmosphere of suspicion, and doddering old Mr. Nosebag takes off his beard, revealing he is the dead man.

Even within the few pages describing *Bezel* there are a number of Nabokovian clues dropped here and there. The most blatant of these is the verbal play with the dead man's

2. *The Real Life of Sebastian Knight* (Norfolk, Conn.: New Directions, 1959), 91–92. (All subsequent quotations from the novel are followed by page numbers in parenthesis.) These pages contain as succinct and telling comments about the moral value of parody as one finds in Nabokov's work. The "opinions" are, of course, Sebastian's, but in this instance I believe he agrees with his creator.

name: G. Abeson read backwards is Nosebag. From the beginning of the narrator's summary one ought to have some idea what will eventually happen. Further, the dead man is an art dealer, and when the inspector arrives and begins to sniff Nosebag's possible guilt he says, adopting a Cockney accent, "'Ullo, 'ow about Hart?" This question introduces a level above the level of detection. It suggests art is the culprit, which turns out to be true. Art *has* murdered Mr. Abeson, and resurrected him in old Nosebag. The game proceeds, obviously, but with a new dimension: the imagination is capable of giving life to the dead, including the form of the detective story. The general parallels to *The Real Life* are clear. Just as G. Abeson lives on in old Nosebag, so Sebastian Knight lives on in his half brother, who says at the end of the novel, "I am Sebastian Knight." Just as the style of *Bezel* becomes more realistic as the novel progresses, so *The Real Life* gradually becomes more realistic as the narrator gets on with his search for information about Sebastian: for twelve chapters the narrative technique is a mixture of accounts of the present search the narrator is undertaking and a series of flashbacks, roughly chronological, about scenes from Sebastian's life. During these twelve chapters one has to exert unusual attention to keep the time pattern straight, and there are strange occurrences, such as the voice in the mist the narrator hears while he is talking to Sebastian's college friend at Oxford. But beginning with Chapter 13 this somewhat riddling alternation disappears for a while, and the narration is given almost entirely to the present. The next five chapters focus on the narrator's search for the woman who was at Blauberg with Sebastian, and, excepting the brief, impressionistic data about Sebastian's romance at sixteen with the sister of a schoolmate, this five-chapter section is a story in itself. But, in Chapter 18, the narrator returns to his original technique and takes it a bit further, turning the story, as he admits, into a dream. Finally, regard-

3

ing these general similarities, the change from boarding house to country house and the discoveries of the characters' complex kinships in *Bezel* parallel, in *The Real Life*, the gradual discovery of Nina Rechnoy's identity at the country house of Madame Lecerf in Chapter 17. In this particular case the narrator learns that what seems to be two people—Nina Rechnoy and Madame Lecerf—is really one.

Other, less explicit self-mating relationships in Nabokov's book correspond with the general interweaving of people which Sebastian Knight accomplished in *The Prismatic Bezel*. For example, Nina Rechnoy herself is the spiritual "sister" of an earlier person to whom Sebastian was attracted, Natasha Rosanov, the sister of Sebastian's school chum in Russia. Her initials are the same as Nina's; moreover, the narrator chooses to put his account of the earlier romance (with Natasha in 1916) in the section of his book dealing with Nina, whom Sebastian loved in 1935. As the narrator says, "There seems to have been a law of some strange harmony in the placing of a meeting relating to Sebastian's first adolescent romance in such close proximity to the echoes of his last dark love. Two modes of his life question each other and the answer is his life itself" (SK, 137). Furthermore, we learn that the fat uncle who is playing chess with Paul Rechnoy has once been a part of Nina's life, and that Paul himself has been Nina's husband. We also become aware that Nina has been impersonating Madame Lecerf, and, as far as *we* know anyway, may *be* Madame Lecerf. What's in a name? Thus, in these and later chapters of *The Real Life* as in Sebastian's own first novel, we discover relationships and identities which have been hidden.

These are three ways, then, that *The Real Life of Sebastian Knight* resembles one of Sebastian Knight's own books: in the parody of detective fiction that becomes a springboard for an idea about the power of the imagination, in the change of style of narration as various discoveries about the interrelationship

4

of characters occur, and in the nature of those interrelationships themselves.

But these are general parallels; the narrator, in summarizing *The Prismatic Bezel*, admits that he has necessarily left out the flavor of the book. "I have tried my best," he says, "to show the workings of the book, at least some of its workings. Its charm, humor and pathos can only be appreciated by direct reading" (SK, 12). For direct reading, of course, we would have to have a copy of the novel, which doesn't exist. In lieu of that book, however, we have its counterpart, *The Real Life*, in our hands, and we encounter there "the charm, humor and pathos" of *Bezel*. The minute and devious ways Nabokov includes in his book what the narrator can't give us from Sebastian's are extraordinary, and reward detailed examination, for what the narrator says about Knight's compositional methods applies to Nabokov's as well:

> Sebastian Knight had always liked juggling with themes, making them clash or blending them cunningly, making *them* express that hidden meaning, which could only be expressed in a succession of waves, as the music of a Chinese buoy can be made to sound only by undulation. . . . It is not the parts that matter, it is their combinations. (SK, 176)

What I want to suggest might be clearer if I begin, more traditionally than the novel entitles me to, with characters. I have tried to give some idea of the spiritual relationship between Natasha Rosanov and Nina Rechnoy, which Nabokov suggests by giving them the same initials, and by juxtaposing near the end of the novel their affairs with Sebastian. But he establishes in the earliest chapters of the book the patterns of which these two characters are a part. For example, in Chapter 2, when the narrator is trying to present a picture of Sebastian's youth, he says that at sixteen Sebastian wrote verses in a black notebook he kept locked in a drawer. The narrator, who was ten at the time, discovers where Sebastian keeps the key, and one day

5

looks in the drawer. He finds, among other items, "the photograph of a sister of one of his schoolmates." This is a photo of Natasha, and its discovery seems the logical place for an account of Sebastian's relationship with her. But, fortunately, the logic of *The Real Life* is not the logic of chronology, and the place for this account is dictated by something time doesn't control. We see immediately that the real life of a man is not a series of events arranged according to a predictable formula. As Madame Lecerf says in another context, "Je ne suis pas le calendrier de mon amie."

Since Nina Rechnoy is a more important person in the life of Sebastian Knight than is Natasha Rosanov, the pattern which Nabokov establishes for her to step into is more elaborate. He begins to establish this pattern early in the book, also. In Chapter 4 the narrator is going through Sebastian's belongings. He burns the two packets of letters as he had been instructed, without reading them; but as a page begins to go up in flames he glimpses a Russian phrase, which he translates "thy manner always to find." These letters are written by Nina and are our first introduction to her place in Sebastian's life. Moreover, the particular phrase the narrator reads sounds the note of a major motif of the novel, discovery, which was Sebastian's manner and is the narrator's obsession. Further, the nature of the narrator's activity when he sees the phrase on the letter is similar to the nature of his activity when he discovered the picture of Natasha: he is going through Sebastian's personal possessions. This serves as another link between the two women and is another illustration that "it is not the parts that matter, it is their combinations." The next allusion to Nina occurs in Chapter 12 and is again in connection with the letters she wrote Sebastian. And, of course, it is with this chapter that Nina begins to emerge as a person in the novel.

But both Nina and Natasha are themselves part of a larger pattern into which all the women in Sebastian's life fit, a pattern which generates insight into Sebastian as a lover. The center of this web is Sebastian's mother, who appears only once in the novel, and is characterized as "a strange woman, a restless reckless being—but not my father's kind of restlessness. . . . Hers was a half-hearted pursuit, capricious and rambling, now swerving wide off the mark, now forgetting it midway, as one forgets one's umbrella in a taxicab" (SK, 8–9). After she leaves Sebastian's father she wanders about Europe, abandoned, feverish, and alone, and finally dies of heart disease in a town called Roquebrune. About three and a half years later her husband, Sebastian's father, is killed in a duel over Virginia Knight's honor. This seems senseless to the narrator, but he tells us that after Sebastian had learned of it he seemed to respect his father much more than he had while the man was alive. This response to his father's fatal actions—in effect, he dies because of a woman—reveals that Sebastian felt strongly about his mother.

Other details support this. On her visit to Sebastian in 1908 Virginia Knight gave him a box of sugar-coated violets. One of the objects that the narrator finds in the locked drawer where Sebastian keeps his notebook is a small muslin bag of violet sweets; the name of the pensione where Sebastian goes and meditates, thinking it is where his mother died, is *Les Violettes*; in the bathroom of Sebastian's apartment in London the narrator finds only a talc tin, but it has violets printed on it, and those violets are reflected in a mirror; the words that Clare Bishop types as Sebastian dictates them to her are black and violet; the narrator looks closely at Madame Lecerf just before she betrays her other identity and see sharply her violet eyelids; finally, on the train to Sebastian's bedside the narrator sees a violet-blue night-lamp reflected in the black window beside him. In all but the last two of these instances, violets, either the color or the flowers, refer to Sebastian's fondness for them. The association is not only with Sebastian's memory of his

7

mother, the focus I began this list with, but also with the appearance of his writing, his art. But in the last two examples—Nina's eyelids and the night-lamp—violet is associated with the narrator. These instances occur very near the end of the novel, near the end of the narrator's quest that culminates with his realization that he has become Sebastian Knight. That is, the pattern involving violets reveals the importance of Sebastian's mother in *his* life and art, and this importance continues after Sebastian's death by becoming a part of the narrator's, in whom Sebastian lives on.

Perhaps more obvious than this is the behavioral similarity between Sebastian's mother and Natasha and Nina. As Virginia Knight was reckless and restless, deserting Sebastian's father almost at whim, so Natasha's love for someone else results in her rejection of Sebastian. The pattern of rejection is, of course, repeated in Sebastian's affair with Nina, who gets rid of him by using another man as her intermediary. In short, Sebastian actively loves two women in his life—Natasha and Nina—both of whom are echoes of his mother, insofar as we come to know his mother.

One more point in this connection: Sebastian takes as his last name the last name of his mother—we never know the Russian name that the father gave to his two wives. Virginia Knight is always spoken of as Knight. Her first name is a Roman *gens*; that is, the name of a clan which reckoned descent through the male. The suggestion is that she is prototypical Knight, Virginia Knight, and that when Sebastian shows his interest in her he is really revealing such an interest in himself. The violets on the talc tin reflected in the mirror, and the night-lamp reflected in the train window, suggest this gently. Perhaps it would be more accurate to say that in his love affairs with his memory of his mother, and with Natasha and Nina, he is seeking the sources of himself. Here, as in other instances, one gets an idea of how the game Nabokov is playing

8

gradually moves into a realm of more complex and important implications.

In my discussion thus far of the women in Sebastian Knight's life, and in the narrator's life, I have not mentioned Clare Bishop on purpose, because Clare's position in the pattern of the real life of Sebastian Knight is somewhat different from the trio of other women I have been talking about. Her name, first of all, suggests her role: one who sees clearly, or, in connection with her duties as Sebastian's secretary, oversees clearly. She is a practical woman, capable of doing what Sebastian is constitutionally incapable of, and as such is very much Sebastian's opposite. Further, she just appears in Sebastian's life, and then, as quietly and unobtrusively, disappears from it, without, in either case, seeming to have any profound effect on him. Certainly not the kind of effect Nina Rechnoy has had. And yet, Clare's letters were in the drawer of Sebastian's London flat along with those from Nina, and the two packets were burned together. And yet (again) the chance meeting the narrator has with Clare on the street, during which she touches the key to Sebastian's apartment, serves as the narrator's inspiration to write his next chapter, in which Clare plays a central role. And the letter from Sebastian's second book, *Success*, seems to the narrator to be addressed to Clare, though disguised by art to seem a part of the novel.

Perhaps I should recapitulate, lest I get lost in the details of my attempt to mirror here, though more mechanically, the arrangement of parts of Nabokov's book. First, the basic idea: the novel as game, in which certain details and people are combined so that the resulting pattern *is* the novel's meaning. (I say details *and* people because of Sebastian's idea in *The Prismatic Bezel*, which I will discuss later, that his characters are methods of composition, themselves parts of a whole picture.) Second, a small pattern: the relationship between Nina Rechnoy and Natasha Rosanov. Third, a wider pattern: the rela-

9

tionship between these two women and Sebastian's mother, which begins to reveal Sebastian's search for himself through them. Fourth, a still more inclusive pattern: to the group of similar people—Virginia, Natasha, Nina—is added a different kind of woman, Clare Bishop, with whom Sebastian spent no less than six years of his life, and who was closer to him as a writer than any other person. Though different in character from the other women with whom Sebastian is involved, Clare Bishop is just as important to the "real life" the narrator is trying to present. This more inclusive pattern begins to suggest that Sebastian is attracted to women who are like himself—wandering, restless—and a woman who is practical, contained, secure. Paradoxically, the women who are wild and reckless—the last of whom may have ruined his life—care nothing about art, while Miss Bishop seems clairvoyant about what Sebastian is trying to express, offering him phrases which he accepts, having failed himself to get them exactly as he wants them. The further implication is that Sebastian is more ardently drawn to women like Nina Rechnoy, since he leaves Clare for her. But, in the process of continuing revision of judgment that this novel asks of its reader, the larger pattern casts doubt on this implication, for the letter which Sebastian writes to his half brother just before he dies reveals a desire for the obvious and the ordinary.

In addition to Sebastian's women another character is important in Nabokov's conception of the novel as a game of arrangement and detection, Herr Silbermann. He appears briefly to assist the narrator when it becomes clear that without unforeseen help he will have to leave the details of Sebastian's last affair out of his book. Silbermann's appearance occupies only nine pages of the story, but he is connected in a number of ways with many important things in other parts of the novel, and in this way can be said to be present often as part of a pattern even when he is not present "in person." One of the first things one notices about Silbermann's meeting with the narrator is the uncanny way they understand each other. Silbermann asks the narrator if he is a traveler. The narrator says he is. Silbermann then asks, "In what?" "Oh, in the past, I suppose," the narrator replies. Silbermann nods "as if he understood." A little bit later this exchange takes place.

"I want to write a book about [Sebastian]," I continued, "and every detail of his life interests me."
"What was he ill?" Mr. Silbermann asked huskily.
"Heart," I replied.
"Harrt,—dat's bad. Too many warnings, too many... general... general... "
"Dress rehearsals of death. That's right."
"Yes."[3]

Silbermann understands the narrator, and the narrator is able to complete Silbermann's meaning for him. Yet it seems they are perfect strangers. One of the few Russian phrases Silbermann remembers is "dear brother" and he gives the narrator a brand new notebook in which the narrator begins writing part of his book about Sebastian.

Silbermann's speech is also arresting; English is not his native language, and the way he speaks it echoes two other manipulations of language in the novel. Here is, first of all, a sample of Silbermann's groping for words.

"Dat is Flambaum and Roth, great fabric, factory. Paper."
"But earlier... last year, four last years, I was in de police—no, no, not once, not quite.... Plain clotheses. Understand me?" (SK, 129–27)

Then the narrator's thoughts later as he rides a train to St. Damier, where Sebastian is either dead or dying.

What on earth was the name of that sanitorium? It began with an 'M'. It began with an 'M'. It began with an... the wheels

---

3. Nabokov's spelling of Silbermann's pronunciation ("harrt") echoes the inspector's question in *The Prismatic Bezel*, thus establishing a second context in which this exchange resides.

> got mixed up in their repetitive rush and then found their
> rhythm again.... Yes, Starov would know where he was.
> Mar... Man... Mat... Would I get there in time?...
> Would I arrive in time to find him alive... arrive... alive...
> arrive... (SK, 192)

And finally this passage:

> As he a heavy A Heavy sleeper, Roger Rogerson, old Rogerson
> bought old Rogers bought, so afraid Being a heavy sleeper, old
> Rogers was so afraid of missing tomorrows. He was a heavy
> sleeper. He was mortally afraid of missing tomorrow's event
> glory early train glory....(SK, 39)

This is the only example of Sebastian Knight's early drafts of
his fiction.[4] The point should be clear on the basis of the han-
dling of language alone: Silbermann is Sebastian is the narrator is Silbermann and so on. In addition, Silbermann and
the narrator are both riding on trains when they speak this way,
which complements the subject matter of Sebastian's frag-
ment. Moreover, old Rogers is afraid of missing a train because he is a heavy sleeper, and the narrator almost misses his
stop on his way to Sebastian's bedside because he keeps falling
asleep.

This is not all. Sebastian wrote three short stories, the last of
which, "The Back of the Moon," is the narrator's favorite. The
story contains a Mr. Siller, who the narrator thinks "is perhaps
the most alive of Sebastian's creatures." Mr. Siller has bushy
eyebrows, a mustache, a bobbing Adam's apple, a big nose,
and a shiny bald head. The description of Mr. Silbermann repeats every one of these details. Besides the similarity of their
appearances, Silbermann's advice to the narrator recalls Mr.
Siller, and the story in which he appears: "'I have made dis,'
he said, 'because you are to me sympathetic. But ... (he
looked at me with mild appeal in his bright brown eyes) but

---

4. Sebastian's odd pronunciation and phrasing when he spoke English (SK, 48)
echoes Silbermann, too.

please, I fink it is ewsyless. You can't see de odder side of de moon. Please donnt search de woman. What is past is past'" (SK, 132). Finally, in Sebastian's story Mr. Siller helps three travelers at a train station; although Mr. Silbermann in *The Real Life* seems to help only one, the narrator, he also helps Sebastian, and himself.

If this interpenetration of identities is mystifying, the following passage, to which I will refer in more detail later, clarifies them. In it the narrator makes explicit the main lesson he has learned from his experience with the real life of Sebastian Knight: "Whatever his secret was, I have learnt one secret too, and namely: that the soul is but a manner of being—not a constant state—that any soul may be yours, if you find and follow its undulations. The hereafter may be the full ability of consciously living in any chosen soul, in any number of souls, all of them unconscious of their interchangeable burden" (SK, 204–205). The interpenetration of Sebastian, the narrator, Siller, and Silbermann embodies this secret and enables the narrator to articulate it at the novel's end. Again, what is partly a game Nabokov orients toward another, more complicated concern. I will return to this particular focus in part II.

Up to now I have been, for convenience, working with characters as illustrations of the similarity between Sebastian Knight's first book and the book which contains its pathos and humor. Other things, too, are integral to this pursuit, as I have suggested in connection with violets, Natasha's photograph, and Silbermann's notebook.

To begin, as Adam did, with names, Sebastian's last one offers a clue to aspects of his identity. It is, first of all, a pun on "n-i-g-h-t," and is spelled this way at least once in the novel, when the narrator is trying to communicate with the man at the hospital desk in St. Damier. This placement of the pun causes a primary association between night and death. The major concern of Sebastian's last novel, *The Doubtful As-*

phodel, is death; the subject of the book is a dying man. Even in Sebastian's second novel, *Success*, the character William has been intensely aware of his own mortality, as the one quoted passage from that book indicates. Moreover, Sebastian's fascination with violets may be connected with death, for violet is the shortest light ray in the spectrum, and the next "color" is black.

Secondly, a knight is a chessman, and we learn early in the novel that Sebastian signed his youthful poems with the figure of a chess knight, black. A knight moves on the chessboard jaggedly, forward and to the side, the pattern of his moves resembling a series of *L*'s. His progress is always qualified by that crablike side movement; it is never directly forward or lineal, as are the moves of all the other pieces. In this context Sebastian's conception in his second novel of the movement of "two lines of life" is revealing: "The two lines which have finally tapered to the point of meeting are really not the straight lines of a triangle which diverge steadily towards an unknown base, but wavy lines, now running wide apart, now almost touching" (SK,97). This irregularity is analogous to the movement of a knight, and Sebastian's wanderings, which, of course, the narrator follows in *The Real Life*.

Thirdly, Nabokov uses a black chess knight as an object at various other times in the novel. In the narrator's search for the woman who had vacationed at Blauberg, he visits the home of Paul Rechnoy. When he meets the narrator at the door Paul is holding a black chess knight. As the two men enter the living room of the apartment, Paul throws the black knight down on the table, on which a chess game is in progress, and its head comes off. Nabokov's gamesmanship is at its most suggestive here. The black knight in Paul Rechnoy's hand lets the reader know that the narrator's search should end here, that Paul's first wife is indeed the woman who threw Sebastian's life into such disorder. The result of throwing the knight on the table is a beautiful image of what happened to Sebastian: he lost his head over Nina. (Part of the pleasure is in the kitsch.) It is similarly revealing that the large and silent man who is Paul's opponent picks up the knight and screws its head back on. It is this man who will be the narrator's key to Nina's identity later on, when she mentions that she once kissed a man because he could write his name upside down. That is, because of this man who puts the knight's head back on, the narrator is able to fit another piece of his puzzle into the larger pattern at the country estate of "Madame Lecerf."

Fourthly, the chess knight returns in the novel as a device through which Nabokov can establish relationships. In the narrator's description of Sebastian's last novel he speaks of the lives of various people who appear in the book as commentaries on the main subject, a dying man. One of these lives is part of the black knight pattern ultimately related to Sebastian's last name: "We follow the gentle old chess player Schwarz, who sits down on a chair in a room in a house, to teach an orphan boy the moves of a knight" (SK, 175). The scene is reminiscent of Sebastian sitting in that lonely hotel after his mother's death, and of Paul Rechnoy's chess opponent, who showed more interest in a little boy and a knight than he did in either Rechnoy or his visitor. This second echo sounds again in the name given the chess player, Schwarz, German for *black*. The narrator, since there were no introductions, has called the other man at Rechnoy's "Black," because he is playing with the black pieces.

In this instance the implications are rather uncanny. It is impossible for Sebastian to have known and included in his book the scene which the narrator was part of at Paul Rechnoy's apartment. Maybe, one thinks, the scene involving the narrator had been commonplace for Sebastian, but Sebastian never *knew* Paul Rechnoy, nor is it sensible to imagine that he would have visited Nina when the rest of the family was around. Very strange—until one remembers that one theme of the novel, and a lesson the narrator learns, involves the interpenetration of souls. Who, the whole procedure asks again, *is* Sebastian Knight, anyway? Well, among other people, he is the narrator traveling the convolutions of the real life of someone else who responds to the same name. In other words, the life which the narrator mentions from Sebastian's last book is autobiographical in two ways: it calls attention to the writer Sebastian Knight by means of the chessman and the name of the player, Schwarz; and it places us in the uneasy realm of the interpenetration of identity that is a subject of *The Real Life*, focusing on the similarity between the subject of the writer's book and the events of the narrator's life.[5] Again, as in

5. Sebastian Knight wrote fiction: three novels, three short stories; he also wrote an autobiography, *Lost Property*. I have noted, too, the recurrent suggestion that his novels themselves are disguised autobiographies. And, of course, the novel I am discussing is titled *The Real Life* of the man; it purports to be a biography of the writer of partly autobiographical novels—hence the narrator feels moved on various occasions to quote from Sebastian's fiction to illustrate points about his life. This is, primarily, all part of Nabokov's concern with imaginative art, which I will focus on in Chapter Two.

There is another direction one might follow here, if one is so inclined. I will point down the thorny path, as it were, but I don't propose to linger there very long myself before abandoning it.

The parallels between Nabokov's life and the life of Sebastian Knight are striking. Sebastian was born in 1899; so was Nabokov. Sebastian was forced to flee his native Russia because of the revolution; so was Nabokov, and the emigrations took place in the same year, 1918. Sebastian left for England to become a student in 1919; so did Nabokov, leaving Russia by way of Sebastopol in the Crimea, an obvious echo of Sebastian's name (though Sebastian's family leaves Russia via Finland). Nabokov's account of his own experiences at Cambridge (SM, Chapter 13) tally remarkably with the data given about Sebastian by his former college friend. Sebastian's vocation is also Nabokov's, and as I have been trying to demonstrate there are similarities between Knight's novels and this particular one by Nabokov; moreover, most of Nabokov's novels deal with "reality" in much the same way *Sebastian Knight* does.

Further, one can't help noticing the way Sebastian greets his half brother in that café in Paris when the narrator first meets Clare Bishop. Sebastian calls his half brother by his initial, "V". Finally, in one of the most poignant moments in *Speak, Memory* Nabokov refers to his older (by ten and one-half months) brother Sergey: "For various reasons I find it inordinately hard to speak about my other brother. That

every case in this novel, we begin with a game and are led to other considerations. But the atmosphere of the game never wholly dissipates.

II   THE NOVEL AS QUEST

The novel-as-game parodies detective fiction; it involves the reader in much the same way a Sherlock Holmes or Nero Wolfe tale involves him, making him pay attention to the smallest details because the clue to the puzzle's solution might be included in one of them. But the fiction of Nabokov and Knight differs from detective fiction in two important ways: first, the stress is on the combinations of the details of the pattern that develops, not on the mysteriousness of the pattern; and second, the game of detection is directed beyond itself. In *The Real Life of Sebastian Knight* the highest region of serious emotion is the region in which a man searches for his identity, the region of the question "Who am I?" and the book is therefore both a game and a quest for self-knowledge. It is no secret, of course, that in Nabokov's novels the line between game and serious quest is never clearly drawn, because his belief seems to be that the point at which the one merges into the other is never precise. The game of detection and the quest for knowledge of one's self are both puzzles, and in both the greatest demand is made on one's attention; in both the minutest detail, the detail that seems to be of least importance, may hold the key to solution. The following passage, which is a combi-

---

twisted quest for Sebastian Knight (1940), with its gloriettes and self-mate combinations, is really nothing in comparison to the task I balked in the first version of this memoir and am faced with now" (SM, 257).

One could play a number of interpretive cards at this point, all jokers (*e.g.*, the novel is a mode of psychological exorcism; the novel is the creation of an alternate reality, an "escape," etc.) As far as I'm concerned there is a large darkness here, or a gambler who has already shown the hand he wants played. To reach up his sleeve is intriguing, yes, but finally jejune. To alter the phrase of another man prying into secrets, and divert his meaning significantly, "The novel's the thing."

nation of quotes from Sebastian's last novel and comments by the narrator, focuses this idea precisely.

> The answer to all questions of life and death, "the absolute so-
> lution" was written all over the world he had known: it was like
> a traveller realising that the wild country he surveys is not an
> accidental assembly of natural phenomena, but the page in a
> book where these mountains and forests, and fields, and rivers
> are disposed in such a way as to form a coherent sentence; the
> vowel of a lake fusing with the consonant of a sibilant slope; the
> windings of a road writing its message in a round hand, as clear
> as that of one's father; trees conversing in dumb-show, making
> sense to one who has learnt the gestures of their language . . .
> Thus the traveller spells the landscape and its sense is disclosed,
> and likewise, the intricate pattern of human life turns out to be
> monogrammatic, now quite clear to the inner eye disentangl-
> ing the interwoven letters. And the word, the meaning which
> appears is astounding in its simplicity: the greatest surprise
> being perhaps that in the course of one's earthly existence, with
> one's brain encompassed by an iron ring, by the close-fitting
> dream of one's own personality—one had not made by chance
> that simple mental jerk, which would have set free imprisoned
> thought and granted it the great understanding. Now the puzzle
> was solved. "And as the meaning of all things shone through
> their shapes, many ideas and events which had seemed of ut-
> most importance dwindled not to insignificance, for nothing
> could be insignificant now, but to the same size which other
> ideas and events, once denied any importance, now attained."
> Thus, such shining giants of our brain as science, art or religion
> fell out of the familiar scheme of their classification, and join-
> ing hands, were mixed and joyfully levelled. Thus, a cherry
> stone and its tiny shadow which lay on the painted wood of a
> tired bench, or a bit of torn paper, or any other such trifle out of
> millions and millions of trifles grew to a wonderful size. Re-
> modelled and recombined, the world yielded its sense to the
> soul as naturally as both breathed. (SK, 178-9)

This is the theme of Sebastian Knight's last book, and it is a theme of the Nabokov novel of which *The Doubtful Asphodel* is a part.

I have tried to illustrate how even the smallest and apparently least important detail begins to take on the same size as those incidents which seem most immediately striking. I want now to work with some other details of the same sort, though they are more obvious to begin with; I will begin by taking a cue from the passage I have just quoted. In it the man who is on the verge of learning the absolute solution of all the questions of life and death is compared to a traveler. The particular man in Sebastian's book, however, is inert physically; he is dying. But the narrator makes it clear that it is impossible to tell exactly where he is: "A man is dying, and he is the hero of the tale; but whereas the lives of other people in the book seem perfectly realistic (or at least realistic in a Knightian sense), the reader is kept ignorant as to who the dying man is, and where his deathbed stands or floats, or whether it is a bed at all" (SK, 175). The man's journey, then, is not physical; he doesn't move. His journey is a journey into his own memory, where he is able to see the landscape of his life in the arrangement that suddenly reveals its meaning. This situation—a journey into the past to find a pattern out of which some meaning can emerge—is not simply the dramatic situation of Sebastian Knight's last novel; it is also the dramatic situation of *The Real Life*. The narrator has told Mr. Silbermann that he is a traveler in the past, and frequently the narrator recalls that he is arranging Sebastian's life not according to chronology, but according to the rhythm he feels peculiar to his subject's experience. His subject's experience is, of course, becoming his own experience, so that the rhythms of Sebastian's life are the rhythms of the narrator's life, too.

With this dramatic situation in mind it seems appropriate that railroad trains play an important part in the structure of Nabokov's novel. Early on the narrator, guided by that personal rhythm, reveals that Sebastian had an intense interest in trains.

> From [his mother] Sebastian inherited that strange, almost romantic, passion for sleeping cars and Great European Express Trains, "the soft crackle of polished panels in the blue-shaded night, the long sad sigh of brakes at dimly surmised stations, the upward slide of an embossed leather blind disclosing a platform, a man wheeling luggage, the milky globe of a lamp with a pale moth whirling around it; the clank of an invisible hammer testing wheels; the gliding move into darkness; the passing glimpse of a lone woman touching silver-bright things in her travelling-case on the blue plush of a lighted compartment." (SK, 10)

This early insight into Sebastian's real life underlies the theme of wandering that becomes primary in his experience. Not only is this movement from place to place—from Russia, to Finland, to Cambridge, to Paris, and thence, in his adult years, all over Western Europe—typical of Sebastian's life, it is characteristic of his mother's life, and it is central to the narrator's life as he gathers material for his biography. Sebastian, after all, is an émigré, a man without a homeland, and the source of his identity becomes the landscape of his books as well as the landscape of Europe over which he wanders, and over which the narrator follows him later on. It is necessary, then, that the narrator ride a number of trains himself; two of these train rides are of great importance to the pattern of meaning that is the real life of Sebastian Knight.

I have discussed one of these, the ride from Blauberg to Strasbourg during which the narrator meets Mr. Silbermann: it is on this train ride that the narrator gets information rather miraculously just when he thought he was going to have to give up his search for knowledge about the woman Sebastian had met at the sanitorium. The second train ride, which strikes one immediately as being a key aspect of the novel, is the narrator's trip from Marseilles to Paris, and then from some unidentified spot on the French countryside to St. Damier, where Sebastian lies dying. It is notable that on this feverish trip the narrator is unable to get to St. Damier by any other means than the railroad: the abortive jaunt in the taxicab is humorous but it is also excruciating because it becomes an obstacle to the narrator's purpose instead of an aid. Thus, in one aspect, the train ride which brings the narrator to Sebastian's hospital illustrates the necessity for the narrator to travel as Sebastian would have traveled, to repeat the pattern Sebastian would have followed. To try anything else is to get nowhere. The implication here is fairly clear, I think: the narrator is almost at the end of his quest for some kind of answer. The answer turns out to be that possibly *he* is his half brother; given this direction of the narrator's quest, it seems purposely fitting that he have to employ the means of conveyance that Sebastian himself would have employed.

The way Nabokov presents the second train ride reveals other significances. Primarily, it is handled as a nightmare; it seems to the narrator to be a section of the dream he had had the night before, in which Sebastian had taken his black glove off his bad hand and dozens of tiny little hands had spilled on the floor. The importance reverberates, again, with Sebastian's books. First of all, as the arrival of the inspector in *The Prismatic Bezel* had suddenly thrown that novel back into a rather dreamlike style and atmosphere, so a similar shifting occurs here. The narrator has prepared us for this earlier. In commenting on his placing the episode of Sebastian and Natasha Rosanov out of its chronological order he has said, "A more systematic mind than mine would have placed [it] in the beginning of this book, but my quest had developed its own magic and logic and though I sometimes cannot help believing that it had gradually grown into a dream, that quest, using the pattern of reality for the weaving of its own fancies, I am forced to recognise that I was being led right, and that in striving to render Sebastian's life I must now follow the same rhythmical interlacements" (SK, 137). As the quest of the inspector for the identity of G. Abeson's murderer had taken on the qualities of a dream, so does the quest of the narrator for the true identity of Sebastian Knight. Moreover, this last train ride has an important relationship to both of Sebastian's other novels. It resembles *Success* in that this train ride is finally bringing together two lines of life that have swerved close to each other at times in the past but never quite joined. And it resembles *The Doubtful Asphodel* primarily in the respect that that entire book is given to a quest that takes place in the mind of the dying man, where dreams take place. That is, the gradual movement into the world of the narrator's dreams that characterizes this novel is a movement we witness in the progress of Sebastian Knight's three books of long fiction: as Sebastian seems to have gradually come to believe the truth is in the mind of the seeker, so the narrator of this novel is coming to understand the same thing.

Whenever one encounters a train or a train ride in *The Real Life of Sebastian Knight*, he is, I think, encountering a focus of the theme of the quest for identity. This quest is Sebastian's and the narrator's. For both of them it leads to memory and to dreams, in both of which regions time and space, as the waking mind orders them, are banished, and more revealing arrangements of experience are possible. The narrator's quest has led him to the strange, rhythmic logic of dreams as he gradually approaches the point where the line of his destiny joins the line of his half-brother's destiny. This occurs at the end of the last train ride in the hospital at St. Damier.

Sebastian's quest had led him to the same regions— memory and dreams—and the record of his quest is preserved in his three novels. In these novels, as I have indicated partially, much of what happens is directly relevant to the narrator's experience as he renders it in his own book. Mr. Siller in Sebastian's "The Dark Side of the Moon" appears in the narrator's experience as Mr. Silbermann. The man the narrator calls "Black" in his visit to Paul Rechnoy appears as Schwarz in *The Doubtful Asphodel*. Here is a passage in which the narrator lists other people who are commentaries on the main subject, the dying man, in *The Doubtful Asphodel*.

We follow the gentle old chess player Schwarz, who sits down on a chair in a room in a house, to teach an orphan boy the moves of the knight; we meet the fat Bohemian woman with that grey streak showing in the fast color of her cheaply dyed hair; we listen to a pale wretch noisily denouncing the policy of oppression to an attentive plainclothes man in an ill-famed public-house. The lovely tall primadonna steps in her haste into a puddle, and her silver shoes are ruined. An old man sobs and is soothed by a soft-lipped girl in mourning. Professor Nussbaum, a Swiss scientist, shoots his young mistress and himself dead in a hotel-room at half past three in the morning. (SK, 175)

All but one of these details have appeared already as part of the narrator's experience in his search for Sebastian's real life. Schwarz we have seen. The fat Bohemian woman is Lydia Bohemsky, one of the women on the narrator's list of those who stayed at the sanitorium while Sebastian was there. The man who has luncheon at Madame Lecerf's country house has a grey streak in his hair. The policy of oppression has been implicitly denounced by the narrator in his account of the family's flight from revolution-torn Russia; and the plainclothesman of the narrator's experience is, of course, Silbermann. We see a tall woman step in a puddle as she gets out of her car at Madame Lecerf's; the desk man at the hotel in Blauberg has, to the narrator's bewilderment, mentioned a Swiss couple who committed suicide in his hotel in 1929. The details of Sebastian's books are, in short, transmuted into the details of the narrator's experience, and the narrator's quest for Sebastian through Sebastian's books grows into a quest for himself.

But even at the end of this quest Nabokov slips in a reminder that it maintains the qualities of a game. The lines of life of the narrator and Sebastian Knight merge at a place called St. Damier. *Damier* is French for *chessboard*. If one considers the narrator a pawn during the course of the novel—a little man who is, in a way, being used—then at St. Damier he becomes a knight—"I am Sebastian Knight," he says—a possible achievement in chess. It is intriguing to consider that a chess game is never really completed: the king is never taken. The game reaches a state of perfect balance in which no more movement is necessary. It is conclusive, but it is also inconclusive.

Before the quest issues in that particular stasis, however, one encounters necessary dramatic embodiments of its nature: when the narrator studies the patterns of Sebastian's novels he is studying the patterns of his own life. When he reads Sebastian's books he is reading his own book. When he studies Sebastian he is looking in a mirror and seeing himself. It should be no surprise, given the reflexive quality of the quest the narrator undertakes in Nabokov's novel, that the Narcissus myth, the mirror experience par excellence, should play an important part. The first suggestion of the importance of Narcissus in *The Real Life* occurs when the narrator describes Roy Carswell's painting of Sebastian:

> These eyes and the face itself are painted in such a manner as to convey the impression that they are mirrored Narcissus-like in clear water—with a very slight ripple on the hollow cheek, owing to the presence of a water-spider which has just stopped and is floating backward. . . . The general background is a mysterious blueness with a delicate trellis of twigs in one corner. Thus Sebastian peers into a pool at himself. (SK, 119)

In one of the six quotes taken from Sebastian Knight's autobiography, *Lost Property*, the role that self-awareness, which was Narcissus' curse, played in his life gets sharp focus: "In my case all the shutters and lids and doors of the mind would be open at once at all times of the day. Most brains have their

Sundays, mine was even refused a half-holiday" (SK,67). From the point of view of the painter Sebastian *is* Narcissus, peering at himself in a pool of water, burdened with the continous awareness of himself. Moreover, in the portrait another dimension of this understanding of Sebastian is suggested. The narrator comments on the spider's club-foot; Sebastian's quest for knowledge of himself is a Romantic quest similar to that of Lord Byron. Only three pages before the portrait is described Sebastian's similarity to Lord Byron has been suggested in one of the quotations the narrator takes from Mr. Goodman's biography of Sebastian. Though the narrator disapproves of Mr. Goodman's idea (because it is Goodman's idea) he approves of the same idea when a friend of his, and Sebastian's, comes up with it. Finally, the narrator himself likens his own treatment of Sebastian's affair with Natasha to a dream Byron had. Sebastian's narcissism, then, has something in it of the experience of another figure who mirrored his own life in his literary works.

The first suggestion of the relationship of the Narcissus myth to Sebastian's life has come from someone who tries to depict his understanding of Sebastian. The second comes from Sebastian himself in the form of his last novel, *The Doubtful Asphodel.* An asphodel is, of course, a narcissus; our word "daffodil" is a sort of mispronunciation of asphodel, and a daffodil is a variation of the general plant family of which it is a member. The doubtful asphodel of the novel turns out to be the "asphodel on the other shore." The subject of Sebastian Knight's last novel is a dying man who journeys back through the past as he lies on his deathbed; the lives of the people who appear in the book are commentaries on the dying man, much as the lives of the people who appear in *The Real Life* are commentaries on Sebastian. As the novel draws to its close the narrator says that it seems that the dying man is about to disclose the absolute secret of the questions of life and death. It turns out that the narrator of Sebastian's book, the man who is about to reveal the ultimate answer, hesitates momentarily, wondering if he shall go the whole way on the printed page. During that moment of hesitation, of course, he dies, and the answer is never spoken—"The asphodel on the other shore is as doubtful as ever." Thus, the answer to the riddle of life and death—that ultimately propitious arrangement of events and details so that they all fall into place and assume equal importance—is doubtful, and it becomes clear that this answer is associated with what is mirrored on the far shore. It is only in death that a man sees the true picture of himself.

It is important here to note that the answer, the asphodel on the other shoe, is doubtful, uncertain, *not* unknown.[6] Thus, though the dying man never articulates this answer, the narrator can't help feeling the answer is in the book anyway. "I sometimes feel," he says, "when I turn the pages of Sebastian's masterpiece that the 'absolute solution' is there, somewhere, concealed in some passage I have read hastily, or that it is intertwined with other words whose familiar guise deceived me" (SK, 180). This is, of course, a point that is applicable to *The Real Life*, too, for in Nabokov's novel the narrator arrives too late to hear Sebastian's final words, although he does come up with an important idea of his own. The narrator also says, in his discussion of *The Doubtful Asphodel* that "the (dying) man is the book"; again, the relevance to *The Real Life* is fairly obvious, it seems to me: Sebastian is the book. As it turns out Sebastian is seven books in all, something I will discuss in Chapter Two.

The two major ideas which the use of the Narcissus myth communicates up to this point in the book are: 1) Sebastian Knight's abnormal awareness of himself out of which his books grow, his books becoming pools of water in which he himself

---

6. See my discussion of the spiral in Chapter Five, and section III of Chapter Six.

is mirrored; 2) death seen as a mirror of life—the asphodel on the other shore—in which the attentive observer can find the arrangements of the events, people, and details of his life that will reveal the meaning of that life. Nabokov takes the importance of the Narcissus myth a bit further, however, as the novel draws to its close. In the two instances I have just been discussing the myth is applicable only to Sebastian Knight, the author. But the novel is about the attempt of Sebastian's half brother to find out who Sebastian really was (or is), a quest that turns out to be a quest for himself. Therefore, Nabokov modulates the relationship of the Narcissus myth to Sebastian into the relationship of that myth to the narrator. At the beginning of Chapter 19, when things begin to fall together for the narrator, he comments, "I have managed to reconstruct more or less the last year of Sebastian's life: 1935. He died in the very beginning of 1936, and as I look at this figure I cannot help thinking that there is an occult resemblance between a man and the date of his death. Sebastian Knight d. 1936. . . This date to me seems the reflection of that name in a pool of rippling water" (SK, 183). The year seems a reflection of Sebastian's name in a pool of water, and the narrator sees in the year, then, what he sees in Sebastian's name. It is significant in this connection to note the telephone number the narrator dials to find out where Sebastian is: Jasmin 61-93. Jasmine traditionally blooms in January, the month of Sebastian's death, and the numbers 6193 are the same digits that are used in the date of the year of his death. The narrator, figuratively speaking, is dialing the time of Sebastian's death when he calls up Dr. Starov. Sebastian's death is the mirror of something extremely important for the narrator, and it is not very difficult to see what. It is with Sebastian's death that the narrator discovers who he himself is. His quest comes to its inconclusive conclusion with the statement "I am Sebastian Knight"; he sees himself in his half brother, just as he has progressively seen his own experience, and his own book, in Sebastian's published works. In this same connection, the narrator sees himself twice in reflection on his way, by train, to Sebastian's deathbed. And he reports this, describing his departure from Marseilles after receiving the telegram: "'Sevastian's state hopeless come immediately Starov.' It was worded in French; the 'v' in Sebastian's name was a transcription of its Russian spelling; for some reason unknown, I went to the bathroom and stood there for a moment in front of the looking-glass. Then I snatched my hat and ran downstairs" (SK, 191). This, again, is a prefiguration of what becomes explicit in the last paragraph of the novel.[7]

Just as Sebastian's works are mirrors in which he is reflected, so is Sebastian a mirror in which the narrator sees himself. Consequently, as Sebastian's works mirror Sebastian, they also mirror the narrator; and they mirror the book the narrator writes. The book is a record of the narrator's quest for himself, as I have said, and the use of the Narcissus myth to figure this quest is also a way of evaluating it. For Narcissus was promised a long life as long as he did not know himself; his suicide was bound up with his discovery of his own reflection in that clear, still pool. Self-knowledge is, in one sense, then, destructive; Sebastian Knight dies. But in another sense it is revitalizing; the narrator lives. The subject of Nabokov's book seems to me to be the ability of a man to renew his life through the destruction of part of himself, or, as Sebastian puts it in that important letter to the narrator, written in Russian, through the shedding of one's skins.

The main purport of the Narcissus myth in *The Real Life of Sebastian Knight* is the union of self-knowledge with the death of self and the renewal of the person who has come to know himself, and thus the book leads back into time from the world of memory and dreams. It is significant to realize, also, that

7. One also notices that the narrator's initial is absorbed into the Russian "spelling" of his half brother's name.

this connection of death with knowledge is presented in other scenes scattered throughout the book.[8]

We have seen two of these: the end of the life of the main character in Sebastian's last novel, and the end of Sebastian's own life, at which time the narrator expects some revelation from Sebastian's lips. He has said, very early in the book during his description of his attempts to see Clare Bishop,

> I simply had to see Clare! One glance, one word, the mere sound of her voice would be sufficient (and necessary, absolutely necessary) to animate the past. Why it was thus I did not understand, just as I have never understood why on a certain unforgettable day some weeks earlier I had been so sure that if I could find a dying man alive and conscious I would learn something which no human being had yet learnt. (SK,76)

This sort of thing has happened twice in the novel before the narrator makes these statements. Both of these earlier occurrences involve the narrator's mother. In the first, she tells the narrator about Virginia Knight, giving him for the first time some knowledge of the first of three women of the same character with whom Sebastian is involved. The narrator gets this information only a few months before his mother's fatal operation; his mother is not, of course, on her deathbed when she imparts this knowledge, but he makes it clear that her death is impending, and thus communicates the association of the insights she gives him and death. In the second of these incidents the narrator's mother recounts to him the details of Sebastian's summer with the poet Alexis Pan and his wife, Larissa. This was in the summer of 1917, which we learn later

---

8. Two other allusive noises might be mentioned in relation to the pattern in which the Narcissus myth resides. Sebastian is a Christian saint who showed remarkable resistance to death, and who, in the particular orthodoxy of which he is a part, eventually transcended it. His explicit presence is suggested through "the martyr with the arrows in his side" (SK, 125). In an even more gossamer undulation in the narrative, Madame Lecerf's name may suggest an inversion in the legend of Artemis and Actaeon, with its transformations: "cerf" is French for "hart." (*Pace*, too, Silbermann.)

was the summer immediately following Sebastian's break with Natasha Rosanov. The trip with Alexis Pan illustrates, among other things, that Sebastian seemed to recover from his heartbreak, and it is also the first experience of wandering that Sebastian had. As such it becomes the forerunner of the pattern of much of the rest of his life, and who is to say for sure that his experience with Natasha wasn't the initial cause for his breaking moorings and becoming, to some extent at an early age, a footloose man? And, finally, in this second incident the narrator takes pains to make it clear that his mother gave him this information at a time when her death was imminent. He says, for example, "She and I talked of [Sebastian] fairly frequently, especially in the last years of her life, when she was quite aware of her approaching end" (SK, 28). [9]

The deathbed, or near-deathbed revelation occupies a central place in the quest of the narrator for what ultimately turns out to be the knowledge of who he is, and as such is part of the role the Narcissus myth plays in the book. To close this attempt to suggest what the region of highest emotion consists of in *The Real Life of Sebastian Knight*, let me come at the relationship between death and knowledge from still another angle.

In another of the passages from *Lost Property* which the narrator has occasion to quote, Sebastian describes the trip he took in 1922 to the place where his mother had died, a small town in southern France called Roquebrune. He tells how he finally discovered, after much questioning, the pensione where his mother had been staying at the time of her death; it is called, as I have already mentioned, *Les Violettes*, a name fitting in perfectly with Sebastian's central memory of his mother. Having found the hotel, Sebastian sits in the garden

9. One could add the one appearance of Virginia Knight just before she dies in Roquebrune, and the episode of the key just prior to Clare Bishop's death, evidently in childbirth—that odd, chance meeting of the narrator and Clare on the street.

on a stone bench and tries to imagine how his mother had looked at the sights he sees before him. He writes, "Gradually I worked my self into such a state that for a moment the pink and green seemed to shimmer and float as if seen through a veil of mist. My mother, a dim slight figure in a large hat, went slowly up the steps which seemed to dissolve into water" (SK, 19–20). This dissolving into water evokes the myth of Narcissus, and the evocation suggests that Sebastian is really seeing himself reflected in his vision. This suggestion is fulfilled when he learns that the Roquebrune where his mother had died was in another section of the country, and he had been at the wrong place entirely when he experienced his ecstatic moment.

This occasion, which is located, according to the imaginative logic that the narrator is using to structure his book, early in the novel (Chapter 2), is alluded to once more in the next chapter, in a context that serves to indicate another dimension of its importance. Sebastian made two trips to Paris to visit his stepmother and half brother after he went to Cambridge. The second of these was occasioned by his stepmother's funeral, which took place in 1922. After the funeral is over the narrator reports, "Next day he left for the South of France." It is on this trip to the South of France that Sebastian visits *Les Violettes* and has his vision. Thus, the narrator's imaginative logic puts the funeral of Sebastian's stepmother and Sebastian's trip to Roquebrune in the same year, one happening on the heels of the other. Again, death and knowledge—though this time the "knowledge" is of a different sort; it is the "knowledge" one receives via the imagination—are suggestively yoked.

Moreover, the incident at Roquebrune is echoed at the novel's close when the narrator keeps his vigil outside the door of the dying man Kegan, whom he takes to be Sebastian. Again, the participant thinks he is in a certain place and his imagination works as if that certain place were the right place.

And, as has been the case with Sebastian at Roquebrune, the imaginative experience which has to do with the realization of something through a sort of vision—the narrator never actually *sees* the man whose breathing he is listening to—is valid even after the person who has had it learns of his mistake. The narrator is able to enunciate the importance of his experience in room 36 even though he knows it wasn't Sebastian at all who lay dying a few feet from him.

In both these cases two ideas are inseparably joined. First, the intense imaginative experiences which Sebastian and the narrator have occur in a context of which death is a central part. Second, both visions are projections of the subjective needs of the person having the vision: Sebastian has seen his mother only once that he can remember vividly, and, as the narrator has told us, he can never forget her. His trip to Roquebrune itself reveals his desire to do homage to a person who is important to him, and the intensity of that importance is cemented by the vision he has in the garden. Likewise, the narrator has gone through no little hell to arrive at the hospital at St. Damier in order to hear what Sebastian might have to say to him on the verge of his death. His response to the sound of Kegan's breathing illustrates his own emotional condition, which exists independently of the particular physical context in which it is set. His response is a mirror of himself, in which, Narcissus-like, he becomes aware of precisely who he is.

These two scenes, then, are part of the overall pattern of the relationship between self-knowledge and death that is another region of emotion that Nabokov uses his game of detection as a springboard to. The progress of the novel is the progress of the narrator's quest for the real life of Sebastian Knight, and this quest turns out to be, as I have been trying to illustrate, a quest for himself. The use of the myth of Narcissus serves to reveal this quest and to evaluate it; everywhere the narrator looks he sees a mirror of himself as well as a mirror of Sebastian, and this ubiquitous reminding of his self-awareness is associated with the curse that self-knowledge brought with it to Narcissus. Self-knowledge is, as the myth embodies the idea, a burden, even a tragedy resulting in death. But as Narcissus committed suicide the blood from his wounds fertilized the ground beside him and a lovely flower sprang up. So it is with the narrator of this novel; his knowledge of himself is gained only at the expense of the death of the self he comes to know. Yet he lives on, and Sebastian lives on in him.

But the two incidents that I have been discussing lead one into another dimension of *The Real Life of Sebastian Knight*. Both Sebastian's vision at Roquebrune and the narrator's experience in room 36 of the hospital at St. Damier are imaginative projections of their inner emotional states, and have validity in themselves regardless of the circumstances in which they occur. The two instances seem to ignore the facts, whatever *they* are, and create experience that has to be accounted for in other terms.

TWO

Angles of Perception

"But the angle he chooses and the aspects he notes are totally different from what a serious reader naturally expects from a serious author."

The Real Life of Sebastian Knight as title points in the directions I have been discussing—the novel as game of detection, the novel as quest—and the "clues" that accumulate as the novel progresses lead toward the identity not of a murderer exactly but of a man who has, Narcissus-like, died of self-awareness. They likewise lead to the identity of a man whose life has been transmuted by that process. The mirror in which he observes himself is actually many mirrors, for the narrator gets many flashes of the identity of Sebastian Knight, and of himself, from various sources. A number of these are people who tell him things about Sebastian's life: his mother, Helen Pratt, Nina Rechnoy, Roy Carswell, P. G. Sheldon, the old college friend of Sebastian's at Cambridge. In this respect the characters of *The Real Life* are similar to the characters in Sebastian's first novel, *The Prismatic Bezel*, whom the narrator calls "methods of composition." In *The Real Life* what the characters compose is Sebastian Knight's real life; the narrator's sense (and therefore the reader's) of that life depends in part on the accumulation of scattered bits of data and impres-

35

sions which the characters impart. Sebastian's life is, quite literally, composed, as a painting is composed. The narrator has himself communicated this early in the novel: "It is as if a painter said: look, here I'm going to show you not the painting of a landscape, but the painting of different ways of painting a certain landscape, and I trust their harmonious fusion will disclose the landscape as I intend you to see it" (SK,95). One way of painting the landscape of Sebastian's life is to view him as Helen Pratt viewed him. Another way would be to see him as his stepmother painted him. Each character's ideas of Sebastian are a way of painting the landscape that was his life, and his "real" life is the harmonious fusion of these various methods of composition. [1]

This is reminiscent of Proust, among others, at least with respect to the act of human perception. [2] With Proust, what we have in our minds about another person—what we call knowledge of that person—is really an image we have concocted out of the bits and pieces of his behavior and appearance that we observe. The image we thus form is not the person at all, but our idea of him, and that idea is always misleading because, for one thing, it is of necessity incomplete and external, and, for another, even as we form our image the person himself changes. Whereas Proust dramatized this understanding, Nabokov assumes it and makes it fundamental to the structure of *The Real Life of Sebastian Knight*. Having as-

1. The narrator's statement early in the novel (SK,44) about Sebastian's "inability to fit into . . . any kind of picture" suggests the difficulty of accomplishing this fusion, and prepares for the clause that closes the novel—"perhaps we both are someone whom neither of us knows." This someone is Nabokov, of course, but I reserve this dimension for discussion in connection with another novel in which the context seems more appropriately self-conscious. The conjurer in *The Real Life* makes a brief appearance only (SK,99–100, as a character in *Success*) and he isn't even anagrammatical.

2. Among Sebastian's books is the last volume of Proust's *A la Recherche du Temps Perdu*, and Sebastian himself offers a soupçon of Proustian style in one of his letters (SK,54). Even Goodman makes the connection, albeit at an unintentionally comic distance (SK,116).

sumed that no one person can know another completely, he presents various aspects of Sebastian Knight, aspects seen from various angles by various people who came in contact with Sebastian Knight during his lifetime. And he rings other changes on this basic assumption. First, he collects these various fragmentary perceptions of Sebastian Knight into a composition which is viewed finally from a single perspective, the perspective of the narrator. This appears contradictory, since it is impossible to know a person from a single perspective, but at second glance the contradiction disappears. For the narrator, the person whose perspective we are left with at the novel's end, is Sebastian himself. What he has been collecting are various reflections of himself. Another way of expressing this is to say that Sebastian Knight has no real life apart from the people who compose him, and to pay attention to the conceptions other people have of him is, in the end, to pay attention to himself. In short, Nabokov has taken Proust a step further and turned the fragmentary nature of perception into the source of self-knowledge.

The technique is reminiscent of Proust in another respect, too. It takes Marcel, the narrator of *A la Recherche du Temps Perdu*, most of his life to realize its patterns and to decide to translate onto the printed page the book that has been written within him by reality. Similarly, Sebastian Knight has to die before it becomes possible to present his real life, the patterns of his life in their totality, their harmonious fusion. In both cases a life has to be lived before it becomes the source of a book about itself; in both cases the source of the book is the pattern of various details and relationships out of the subject's past. Just as Sebastian discovers in the last pages of his last book, so Marcel discovers in the last pages of *Le Temps Retrouvé* that what seemed small and trivial is in reality of great importance, and both Marcel and Sebastian (and the narrator of Nabokov's book) learn that all aspects of one's life become balanced in significance when viewed from the end of that life. Nabokov rings one more important modulation on Proust here: the end of a life and the balanced portrait of the landscape that is that life is the beginning of a new life. The old self dies and is known in the same instant—this is the importance of the narrator's dialing Jasmin 61-93, the year of Sebastian's death and his self-realization. The old self is known and dies in the same instant, and in that instant a new self is born. Only if it dies can the seed bring forth its fruit.

All this is true of *The Real Life*, however, only if the novel is viewed from the inside, from the perspective of the narrator. Once one steps outside of the novel—when one is the reader of the novel instead of its narrator—what seems to be a complete and harmonious fusion may, for various reasons, be incomplete and not as harmonious as the narrator seems to think it is. The novel is told from the first-person point of view and the first-person point of view is always suspect. What, and for what reasons, is the narrator minimizing, what does he wish to be left out? Does he interpret or evaluate any data himself, and if so what is the effect of his interpretation on the total picture he is supposedly presenting? What is the reader able to take into account that the narrator tries to dismiss?

What the reader is obliged to take into account that the narrator tries to dismiss completely is the first biography of Sebastian, the one which beat his own work to press and had a very successful sale: *The Tragedy of Sebastian Knight*, by a man who is never called anything but Mr. Goodman. The narrator has little or no respect for either this book or its author; from his first mention of both in Chapter 1 to his abolition of both in Chapter 12, he has nothing good to say about either. He makes a great pretense of being civil in his treatment of his visit to Mr. Goodman in Chapter 6, but his fear of libel is clue enough that his civility is assumed, and very badly assumed, too.

38

The narrator tries to present his rejection of Mr. Goodman's book on grounds of its utterly false presentation of Sebastian's character, but other reasons for his disgust with the first biography of his half brother are unmistakable. A primary one is jealousy.[3] Mr. Goodman beat him to the draw; Mr. Goodman experienced what he never did, four years of close relationship with Sebastian; Mr. Goodman's book was successful (it sold); some of Sebastian's manuscripts were left in Goodman's care (which results in a lawsuit to which the narrator refers later in the novel). But perhaps more basic than any of these causes for the narrator's jealousy is his implicit realization that Mr. Goodman, even though he took an entirely different approach to Sebastian's life, used the same *method* in making his book that the narrator uses in *The Real Life*. This method is, after all, one basic method of biography: the use of passages from the fiction of the author to comment on and reveal his life. It obviously allows the writer of the biography some latitude of interpretation, which is precisely the point. Mr. Goodman's biography is just as imaginative as the narrator's, which is the source of the narrator's intense objection to it.

The evidence for this is carefully included in *The Real Life*. In Chapter 3 the narrator gives us a sample of Mr. Goodman's method: Mr. Goodman quotes a passage from *The Doubtful Asphodel* to support his assertion that Sebastian was glad to have escaped from the developing tyranny of revolutionary Russia. The narrator disagrees with this interpretation, saying that Sebastian remembered Russia with fondness, and goes on to quote another passage, this one from *Lost Property*, to support his disagreement. It is possible to argue, of course, that the narrator's quotation is more trustworthy than Mr. Goodman's because it comes from Sebastian's autobiography; it is

3. One of the most brutal (to the narrator) effects of Goodman's version of Sebastian's life is his own diminution in it: "To readers of Goodman's book," he says, "I am bound to appear non-existent—a bogus relative, a garrulous imposter" (SK,6).

39

not spoken by a character in a novel, as is the passage Mr. Goodman cites. But in other instances, and they are numerous, the narrator uses passages not from the autobiography but from the fiction of Sebastian Knight as if those passages indisputably referred to Sebastian's life. Here are two examples. First, in Chapter 1, the narrator is re-creating as much of Sebastian's childhood as he can. He presents the effect of Virginia Knight's desertion on Sebastian's father:

> I do not like to dwell in mind upon that day in a Paris hotel, with Sebastian aged about four, poorly attended by a puzzled nurse, and my father locked up in his room, "that special kind of hotel room which is so perfectly fit for the staging of the worst tragedies: a dead burnished clock (the waxed moustache of ten minutes of two) under its glass dome on an evil mantelpiece, the French window with its fuddled fly between muslin and pane, and a sample of the hotel's letter paper on the well-used blotting-pad." This is a quotation from *Albinos in Black*, textually in no way connected with that special disaster, but retaining the distant memory of a child's fretfulness on a bleak hotel carpet, with nothing to do and a queer expansion of time, time gone astray, asprawl . . . (SK, 9)

The narrator admits that in the context of the story this quotation has nothing to do with Sebastian's mother's desertion, yet he uses it unabashedly in connection with Sebastian's memory of that incident. Secondly, in his discussion of a fictional passage from *Lost Property*, the narrator quotes a love letter found in the mailbag of a wrecked airplane, and then uses this letter as a mirror of Sebastian's response to the end of his affair with Clare Bishop. In both these cases, as in others, the narrator is employing exactly the same method in his book that Mr. Goodman employed in his. The method works equally well for both men, yet leads to entirely different interpretations of Sebastian.

The similarity in methods of Mr. Goodman and the narrator goes deeper into the fiber of the real life of Sebastian

Knight. Mr. Goodman and the narrator have a similar problem in trying to present the parts of Sebastian's life that they have not directly been involved in, or have trouble remembering. The narrator has trouble with Sebastian's boyhood in Russia.

> Sebastian's image does not appear as part of my boyhood, thus subject to endless selection and development, nor does it appear as a succession of familiar visions, but it comes to me in a few bright patches, as if he were not a constant member of our family, but some erratic visitor passing across a lighted room and then for a long interval fading into the night. (SK, 18)

And Mr. Goodman has trouble with Sebastian's early experiences in England.

> Mr. Goodman was no Boswell; still, no doubt, he kept a notebook where he jotted down certain remarks of his employer—and apparently some of these related to his employer's past. In other words, we must imagine that Sebastian in between work would say: Do you know, my dear Goodman, this reminds me of a day in my life, some years ago, when... Here would come the story. Half a dozen of these seem to Mr. Goodman sufficient to fill out what is to him a blank—Sebastian's youth in England. (SK, 63–64)

Here the narrator objects to Mr. Goodman's method of recreating Sebastian's past, yet it is precisely the method he himself has been forced to use earlier. The point is, of course, that this is the method of the narrator's entire story; *The Real Life of Sebastian Knight* is two hundred pages of collected fragments of the totality of Sebastian Knight's life, pieced together according to some uncanny imaginative rhythm that the narrator trusts implicitly. It is obvious, then, that the stated reasons for the narrator's rejection of Goodman's book are not to be trusted. If they were, then the narrator would have to reject his own book as well, which, of course, he cannot do. From the perspective of the reader of Nabokov's novel, then, the implication is fairly clear: the whole picture of the landscape of

41

Sebastian's life has to include Mr. Goodman's understanding. What the narrator tries to dismiss for reasons which are manifestly nonliterary, and which have little to do with the quest for imaginative truth, must be included by the reader. There is more to Sebastian's real life than the narrator is willing to admit.

But there are contradictions in Mr. Goodman's particular presentation. For example, he writes that Continental Europe "shocked [Sebastian] indescribably by the vulgar glamor of its gambling-hells" (SK, 63). Yet we read in a passage of *Lost Property*: "After Cambridge I took a trip to the Continent and spent a quiet fortnight at Monte Carlo. I think there is some Casino place there, where people gamble, but if so, I missed it, as most of my time was taken up by the composition of my first novel" (SK, 19). Again, if this were all there was to the matter, we might have some reason to dismiss Mr. Goodman's book as inaccurate and untrustworthy. But two instances in the narrator's presentation reveal the same kind of inconsistency. First, after he visits Paul Rechnoy (and misses the clue of the black chess-knight Paul holds in his hand) he thinks to himself, "was not the image Paul Paulich had conjured up a trifle too obvious? The whimsical wanton that ruins a foolish man's life. But was Sebastian foolish? I called to mind his acute distaste for the obvious bad and the obvious good; for ready-made forms of pleasure and hackneyed forms of distress" (SK, 149). He decides that Nina couldn't be the woman whom Sebastian became involved with; it happens that he is wrong. It is interesting, moreover, to remember that only one woman attracts the narrator during the course of his searches, and that woman is Nina Rechnoy.

There is a similar contradiction in Chapter 18. The narrator has just come upon an advertisement for Sebastian's last book in a newspaper, and he has a vision of Sebastian enjoying his success: "I imagined him standing in a warm cheerful room at some club, with his hands in his pockets, his ears glowing, his eyes moist and bright, a smile fluttering on his lips,—and all the other people in the room standing around him, holding glasses of port, and laughing at his jokes" (SK, 181). The projected vision the narrator has at this point is contradicted by much of what we have already learned about Sebastian. It was partly because he could not abide such literary parties that he and Clare Bishop had parted. And later descriptions of his behavior at cocktail gatherings in 1935 show him to be a taciturn man who says nothing at such parties, let alone tell jokes.

As in the earlier instance, the weakness of Mr. Goodman's book is also the weakness of the narrator's, although what the narrator is willing to criticize Goodman for he is unwilling to recognize in his own book. The reader's perspective on the real life of Sebastian Knight is again shown to be greater than the narrator's, and one confronts the same implication again. When one assumes that the real life of a man consists of the various reflections of him in other people, then one has to take into account *all* the reflections he can find; he has no power of selection. Moreover, these reflections may, and in fact do, contradict each other at times, precisely because of the nature of human perception. The image any one person has of another person is in part determined by what the perceiver wants to see. Thus, though the evidence contradicts him, the narrator imagines Sebastian the scintillating center of a cocktail party; thus, though Sebastian's own comments contradict him, Mr. Goodman imagines Sebastian shocked by the gambling-hells of Europe. The chief reason for the narrator's rejection of Mr. Goodman's book gradually becomes clear, I think. He rejects this particular reflection of Sebastian simply because he does not wish to think of Sebastian the way Goodman thinks of him. The truth or falsity of Goodman's vision becomes irrelevant, as do the narrator's ostensible objections to the methods Goodman used in writing his book. But, though the narrator can reject Mr. Goodman's idea of Sebastian Knight, the reader cannot, unless, of course, he rejects the narrator's as well.

And is there, after all, so much difference between the narrator's idea of Sebastian Knight and Mr. Goodman's? Mr. Goodman presents Sebastian in simplistic terms as the isolated twentieth-century artist who cannot find a way out of the confines of his supersensitive soul. He is trapped, so says Goodman, in himself, and cannot connect himself with the world he finds himself living in. Sebastian is, according to Goodman, adrift in the world, and the world he is adrift in is broken and disarranged because of its experience of war. How different is this, finally, from the picture of Sebastian the narrator presents? For him, Sebastian is a wandering émigré, a homeless man whose books become his refuge. These books focus on the fragmented perception of human beings, and are themselves, at least in part, puzzles whose pieces must be carefully put together. Moreover, Sebastian is forever contemplating himself. Though the narrator is given to less crude terms by which to express his understanding of Sebastian, the understanding itself is not really very different from Mr. Goodman's. It is simply that the narrator prefers his terms to Goodman's; he does not wish to think of Sebastian as Goodman does.

I admit that the narrator's idea of Sebastian is more interesting and involving than Goodman's rather glib and simple-minded one. But this is not the point. The subject of the novel is human perception, and the assumption that the novel dramatizes is that human knowledge is an accumulation of fragments, a collection of brief and incomplete reflections, and the only way one arrives at even the hint of a "real" life is to assemble as many reflections as possible. Thus, whether one likes it or not, whether the narrator wants to allow it or not, it is possible to think of Sebastian Knight as a tragic figure, and the possibility of an interpretation of his life as a tragedy must be admitted into the landscape of his character. In a grudging way the narrator himself admits this possibility: "And if only he [Goodman] had not padded and commented these 'curious incidents and fancies' so ponderously, with such a rich crop of deductions! Churlish, capricious, mad Sebastian, struggling in a naughty world of Juggernauts, and aeronauts, and naughts, and whatnots... Well, well, there may be something in all that" (SK,65).[4]

But there is another important aspect of the reader's relationship to *The Real Life of Sebastian Knight* yet to consider. Granted that the characters of the novel are methods of composition, granted that what they compose is the landscape titled Sebastian Knight's life, granted that this landscape is incomplete if Mr. Goodman's idea is discounted as the narrator wants it discounted—given all this, there is still the very nature of this landscape. The real life of Sebastian Knight is a book, an imaginative creation of Vladimir Nabokov, somehow in touch with the narrator, who is called "V". The man Sebastian Knight, as far as a reader can know him at any rate, is this book. And the basis of this book is still other books: Mr. Goodman's *Tragedy of Sebastian Knight*, Sebastian Knight's own three novels, three short stories, and that autobiography, *Lost Property*. In other words, Sebastian Knight is not one but seven books, six of which are included in the one the reader holds in his hands.

The closing passage of Chapter 5 affords a nice entry into this rather shifty world. The narrator has just taken his leave of the old friend of Sebastian's at Cambridge when he hears Sebastian's name called in the distance: "'Sebastian Knight?' said a sudden voice in the mist, 'who is speaking of Sebastian Knight?'" In the best novelistic fashion the chapter ends with

---

4. This "conclusion" is strengthened by the inclusion of Goodman among those "coming and going on the lighted stage" in the novel's last paragraph.

this mysterious voice and one turns the page for the sudden revelation. What he gets instead is this:

> The stranger who uttered these words now approached—Oh, how I sometimes yearn for the easy swing of a well-oiled novel! How comfortable it would have been had the voice belonged to some cheery old don with long downy ear-lobes and that puckering about the eyes which stands for wisdom and humor . . . A handy character, a welcome passer-by who had also known my hero, but from a different angle. "And now," he would say, "I am going to tell you the real story of Sebastian Knight's college years." And then and there he would have launched on that story. But alas, nothing of the kind really happened. That Voice in the Mist rang out in the dimmest passage of my mind. It was but the echo of some possible truth, a timely reminder: don't be too certain of learning the past from the lips of the present. Beware of the most honest broker. Remember that what you are told is really threefold: shaped by the teller, reshaped by the listener, concealed from both by the dead man of the tale. Who is speaking of Sebastian Knight? repeats that voice in my conscience. Who indeed? His best friend and his half brother. A gentle scholar, remote from life, and an embarrassed traveller visiting a distant land. And where is the third party? Rotting peacefully in the cemetery of St. Damier. Laughingly alive in five volumes. Peering unseen over my shoulder as I write this. (SK, 52)

The third party, Sebastian Knight, is "laughingly alive in five volumes." And yet, how is he alive in these five volumes? Note these two passages: "Sheldon thinks that the world of the last book he [Sebastian] was to write several years later was already casting its shadow on all things surrounding him and that his novels and stories were but bright masks, sly tempters under the pretense of artistic adventure leading him unerringly towards a certain imminent goal" (SK, 104). In the second passage the narrator seems to come to share Sheldon's idea: "I fail to name any other author who made use of his art in such a baffling manner—baffling to me who might desire to see the real man behind the author" (SK, 114). Thus, Sebastian's work is a mask behind which he hides himself; yet it is the chief source of his identity. I have already tried to some extent to illustrate how the novel the narrator is composing is itself a mirror of Sebastian's work, and, of course, the narrator is really seeking himself when he seeks the identity of Sebastian. The self is, therefore, an imaginative construct, an artistic composition; and "the light of personal truth is hard to perceive in the shimmer of an imaginary nature."

Note, for example, the description of *Lost Property*, Sebastian's autobiography, in connection with which the narrator has made the statements I have just quoted. In the one passage he gives us from that book we learn of the mixup of two letters: one is a love letter that is found enclosed in an envelope addressed to a man named Mortimer; the other, found in an envelope addressed to a woman, begins, "Dear Mr. Mortimer, In reply to yours of the 6th." The two letters have obviously been written by the same person and then put into the wrong envelopes. This is a fictional incident from Sebastian's autobiography, yet it turns out that the narrator's boss is named Mortimer, and a possible implication is that the narrator has written the letters. What Nabokov suggests here, as he does in so many other places, is the interpenetration of fiction and reality, between which there is, as this novel grows, little if any distinction. The real life of Sebastian Knight is the imaginary life of Sebastian Knight; the real world is the world of the imagination.

This interpenetration of the real and the imaginary is suggested in two ways: the basic way is the mirroring in the narrator's book, and in his life, of Sebastian's books; the other way is through the use of the mask, not simply as it is mentioned in connection with Sebastian the author as opposed to Sebastian the man, but as it appears as an object in *The Real Life*. During the narrator's visit to Mr. Goodman a black mask plays a rather mysterious part in the interview. The narrator

47

opens his account of the meeting this way: "'Pray be seated,' he said, courteously waving me into a leather armchair near his desk. He was remarkably well-dressed though decidedly with a city flavor. A black mask covered his face. 'What can I do for you?' He went on looking at me through the eyeholes and still holding my card" (SK, 57). As the interview progresses the narrator continues to remind us that Goodman has this mask on, and as the narrator leaves this happens: "After shaking hands with me most cordially, he returned the black mask which I pocketed, as I supposed it might come in usefully on some other occasion" (SK, 59). The statement makes it sound like the mask belonged to the narrator originally and that Mr. Goodman, having borrowed it for some purpose or other, returns it to the narrator, who may have some use for it himself. Thus, the three writers in Nabokov's novel all wear masks: Sebastian's work is spoken of as a veil over the man himself; Mr. Goodman, the one time we see him, is wearing a mask; and as he leaves Goodman's office the narrator accepts this mask as though it were his to begin with. And indeed, as the rest of the masquerade dissolves at the book's end, the narrator tells us he cannot stop acting his part, and therefore "the hero remains, for, try as I may, I cannot get out of my part: Sebastian's mask clings to my face, the likeness will not be washed off."

This is not as confused as it may sound. The source of the real life of Sebastian Knight is his work. Yet this work is a mask he wears over his own face. Therefore, anyone who tries to reconstruct the real life of the man is doomed from the beginning to reconstruct the life of his mask, his imaginative life. Likewise, both men who attempt to accomplish this biographical reconstruction wear masks; what they write down will be veils over veils. What one receives from Nabokov's novel is a composition some remove from "the facts," whatever *they* are: there is Sebastian, there is Sebastian with his

48

mask on, and there are Sebastian's biographers busy revising that mask after their own sentimental and rhythmic predilections. There are, then, not simply while the narrator is talking to the Cambridge don but throughout the book, three people (at least) "speaking of Sebastian Knight": Sebastian Knight (the writer we presume), the mask of Sebastian Knight (his books), and Sebastian's biographers. The result is a composite identity that is the novel itself, the arrangement of each version that becomes still another version, and answers to the same name, but in a hall of echoes. It is no wonder that the adverb "laughingly" occupies a key place in the narrator's comments about the voice he hears through the mist.

As in other aspects of this (and every) Nabokov novel, one never entirely escapes the delight and frustration of a challenging and complex game. One is moving in two or three dimensions at once while he reads *The Real Life*, and at no time can he be sure which of them has the familiar and comfortable solidarity of what we like to think of as factual reality. The game consists chiefly in keeping oneself alert enough to follow the shifting perceptions that characterize this fiction; the danger is that one may fall into the trap of thinking that he has found the bedrock of "reality" he is used to and will be content to stand on it. Two or three times in the novel one feels that he is on the verge of having this happen: the voice in the mist almost fools the narrator; it seems for a while that the identity of the woman at Blauberg will be the key to the mystery; Clare Bishop herself for a short time appears to hold some knowledge that will put everything into perspective. Finally, at the novel's end one experiences something like a revelation. The narrator discovers what by this time should be evident. But the narrator's announcement that he is Sebastian Knight is no revelation at all, partly because the whole novel dramatizes this identification, and partly because the problem of who the "real" Sebastian Knight is is not solved at all. He takes off one of his

49

masks—the mask of the half brother who has narrated this tale—but what does one find underneath? Another mask. For to identify himself as Sebastian Knight is the same thing as the narrator's saying, "Look, I am not only alive in five volumes, I am also alive now in this one you have just been reading." And, though the narrator would not admit it, he is also alive in Mr. Goodman's book, but masked there, too, as he is everywhere else.

Playing this game of masks and mirrors is fun. It has been criticized by some as being no more than that. Some people think that playing the game is not even fun; like the businessman the narrator asks about Sebastian's books, they are not interested in seeing where their puzzlement and frustration might lead them. A friend of mine, who had read all of Nabokov's books before *Ada* appeared, told me after he had bumped his face on that monument, "Well, he's just like those other Russians after all—a classic bore." With this sort of response in mind, it is possible to take the narrator's attitude toward Sebastian's work when one evaluates Nabokov's fiction: "I don't know whether it makes one 'think,' and I don't much care if it does not. I like it for its own sake" (SK, 182).

As it happens, I do, but by itself that is a simplistic and defensive attitude. Nabokov's novels *do* make one think, for what that is worth; the point is that they do not make one think in the terms to which one is habituated.[5] They force one to come at problems from a different angle; like Sebastian himself, Nabokov uses the novel-as-game as a springboard to higher regions of emotion. He knows how to combine serious concerns with utter delight, which is to say he practices the substantial distinction between what is serious and what is solemn. The epithet "tragicomic" is at a slight distance from describing his

5. The notion defies the dictionary, but I think what most people mean by "boredom" is the fright they experience when they encounter the possibility they may have to change a habit.

fiction because he is too willfully perverse and bizarre. But always for a purpose, at least partly to jar his reader out of habitual modes of response to the world and lead him back into it with a fresh vision.

What are the serious concerns of *The Real Life of Sebastian Knight?* I have tried to suggest some of them. They are not very different from the concerns of writers we return to again and again: the poignance of exile and loss; the immeasurable difficulty of believing that anything, especially memory, touched by time can be trustworthy; the impossibility of returning not just to a place but to a moment; and the terrible chance that other people's lives, as glimpses of them suggest, may be more substantial than one's own.

I would reiterate one other in particular, the reality of the imagination, not only that the imagination exists, but that reality cannot be thought of as existing apart from it. If it is a critical commonplace to say that the act of perception involves both perceiver and perceived, and the knowledge gained from perception is a combination of what one might call "facts" (what is perceived) and imagination (the inventive disposition of the mind of the perceiver), it is not a popular one, even today. It is impossible to know anything as it is in itself; what one knows is his idea of the thing, a relationship. In this respect, everything wears a mask. In this respect, also, the very act of knowing is the act of being deceived. Because of his presence in Sebastian's library, I have already alluded to Proust in a similar context. Here again, Nabokov waves to him as he enters the penumbra. There is no doubt in the mind of the narrator of *A la Recherche* that he exists, and that the aspects of his past that reassert themselves in his present exist, though the pattern they have written into his life is apprehensible subjectively only. He believes in the succession of selves that he realizes has been his life.

In Nabokov's novel this certainty is called into question. As the Narcissus myth especially suggests, what a human being knows is himself, and since everything external to him is only a reflection of himself, what is to convince him of his own reality? The narrator of *The Real Life* says he is Sebastian Knight, and yet this is to admit that he is a man whom he cannot know, except as he projects imaginative ideas of him. The value of self-knowledge is debatable when it is looked at in this way, and since self-knowledge is the last step left to a man who can have no knowledge of anything else, it becomes a kind of death. This complexity is, I think, inseparable from the condition of exile and the image of Sebastian Knight's life as restless wandering. Imaginative composition, particularly of the self, is the only country such a man can truly call his own, and it is full of its own special perils.

Not the least of these is the central price of consciousness, that it can be directed toward itself. Sebastian Knight speaks of the torment of a man whose mind does not take Sunday off. He writes in the letter from *Lost Property*: "Go away, go away. Don't write. Marry Charlie or any other good man with a pipe in his teeth" (SK, 114). Silbermann advises the narrator not to write his book about Sebastian—which is to say one aspect of Sebastian tells another aspect of Sebastian not to try to know Sebastian. Even Goodman, though he appears commercially motivated, advises the narrator not to write his book. And that book, *The Real Life of Sebastian Knight*, ends with this sentence: "I am Sebastian, or Sebastian is I, or perhaps we both are someone whom neither of us knows."

Nabokov affirms this state of affairs.[6] Though man is the

---

6. I mean, of course, the experience of the novel affirms it. In a BBC interview (1969) Nabokov affirmed it outside the context of his novels. In answer to the question, "What distinguishes us from animals?" he replied, "Being aware of being aware of being. In other words, if I not only know that I *am* but also know that I know it, then I belong to the human species. All the rest follows—the glory of thought, poetry, a vision of the universe. In that respect, the gap between ape and man is immeasurably greater than the one between amoeba and ape. The difference between an ape's mem-

only creature who can direct his consciousness toward himself and become Humpty-Dumpty, that burden is also a source of delight, and it is preferable to the other alternative, to have no mind at all.

As I have said, this is matter the novel embodies, presents. It is in the presentation that the imagination performs the primary activity. It creates, and the process itself is fundamentally available in the simple experience of reading the book. Most of my detailed commentary tacitly celebrates this performance through its particulars, while at the same time trying to suggest the formal premise at the source of my own study: that Nabokov invariably conceives his novels both as historically and formally related to certain forebears, *and as something else*. It is the something else—the other mode: game, quest, perceptual puzzle (or assemblage)—which vivifies the form, and I am primarily concerned with its variety. In the following chapters I will consider other modes, but the three I have used *The Real Life* as the occasion for discussing are central to all the other novels as well.

---

ory and human memory is the difference between an ampersand and the British Museum library" (SO, 142).

Perhaps it is appropriate here to carry the distinction between *The Real Life* and its author one step further. I have been focusing the *novel's* emphases in these paragraphs; I assume they are only partial from Nabokov's perspective. He was a lepidopterist, which alone suggests epistemological possibilities *The Real Life* doesn't touch, and the range of his other interests, as the contents of *Strong Opinions* reveal, far surpasses the range of interests of his fictions, and their characters. In this regard *The Gift*, and possibly *Ada*, veer toward the variety and complexity of the man who created them. I think the rest of his fiction occupies itself, variously and to varying degrees, with the sort of perceptual enclosures I have been discussing in this chapter. See also note 2 for Chapter Seven.

THREE

All the Mind's a Stage: The Novel as Play

Nabokov's practice of prefacing the English versions of his Russian novels by disclaiming certain possible interpretive bases for his books is well known. A representative instance occurs in *Bend Sinister*:

> There exist few things more tedious than a discussion of general ideas inflicted by the author or reader upon a work of fiction. The purpose of this foreword is not to show that *Bend Sinister* belongs or does not belong to "serious literature" (which is a euphemism for the hollow profundity and the ever-welcome commonplace). I have never been interested in what is called the literature of social comment (in journalistic and commercial parlance: "great books"). I am not "sincere." I am not "provocative," I am not "satirical." I am neither a didacticist nor an allegorizer. Politics and economics, atomic bombs, primitive and abstract art forms, the entire Orient, symptoms of "thaw" in Soviet Russia, the Future of Mankind, and so on, leave me supremely indifferent. As in the case of my *Invitation to a Beheading* . . . automatic comparisons between *Bend Sinister* and Kafka's creations or Orwell's clichés would go merely to prove

that the automaton could not have read either the great German writer or the mediocre English one. [1]

And on *Invitation to a Beheading* he has this to say:

My favorite author (1768–1849) once said of a novel now utterly forgotten, "Il a tout pour tous. Il fait rire l'enfant et frissonner la femme. Il donne á l'homme du monde un vertige salutaire et fait rêver ceux qui ne révent jamais." *Invitation to a Beheading* can claim nothing of the kind. It is a violin in a void. The worldling will deem it a trick. Old men will hurriedly turn from it to regional romances and the lives of public figures. No clubwoman will thrill. The evil-minded will perceive in little Emmie a sister of little Lolita, and the disciples of the Viennese witch-doctor will snigger over it in their grotesque world of communal guilt and *progresivnoe* education. [2]

It is sensible, I think, to believe what Nabokov says in these prefaces, but at the same time to believe it in the same spirit in which he asks for belief, with a grain of salt in the cheek. To confront this specifically in *Beheading*, it is possible to read the novel as a fantasy based on the working of law in a dictatorship; it is possible, in other words, to consider the novel under two of the modes that Nabokov particularly rejects, allegory and satire. The horror and inhumanity of a tyrannical execution of a person who does not conform is excruciatingly presented: the experience in the courtroom where Cincinnatus C. is sentenced is revoltingly sticky and clearly irrelevant to justice; the thoroughness with which the mentality of tyranny has usurped the minds and sensibilities of the citizens of the state is clear enough, as transparent, in fact, as the citizens themselves; the sense of futility a man experiences whose state, in lawlessly

1. *Bend Sinister* (New York: Time, Inc., 1964), xii.
2. *Invitation to a Beheading* (New York: G. P. Putnam's Sons, 1959), 7. All further quotations will be from this edition, followed by page numbers in parentheses. The "favorite author," also fictitious, is Pierre Delalande, and the quotation, translated, is "It has everything for everybody. It will make the child laugh and the lady shiver. It will give the man of the world a bracing dizziness and make dream the man who never dreams." The epigraph for *Invitation to a Beheading* is "from" his *Discours sur les ombres*: "Comme un fou se croit Dieu, nous nous croyons mortels."

condemning him for being a human being, offers him no recourse in its machinery of law, is agonizing—all paths of escape lead inevitably to one's prison cell in such a political situation. It is even possible to specify the particular nation to
which the allegory could be said to refer. In his usual oblique
way, Nabokov suggests Soviet Russia.[3] For instance, in the
passage concerning the librarian's response to M'sieur Pierre's
card trick (IB,86–87) there are the phrases "red magic" and
"like a sickle"; further, the director's on-the-spot elimination
of the librarian, who has not responded properly to his
superiors, suggests the functioning of power within a tyranny
such as the newly instituted one Nabokov had escaped from
not too long before he wrote this novel. Moreover, it is the
Russian wolfhound (the borzoi) that is named near the end of
the book as the dog image of the soldier's face masks. All this
makes sense, I think, and yet to speak this way of the novel, as
if it were basically a fantasy-satire directed at dictatorial politics, is clearly to limit oneself to only one aspect of the experience the novel affords. These terms omit much of what is
unique in the book: its wit, the density and obliquity of its
style, the suggestions that are made about the nature of experience in *any* political organization, as well as the role that such
themes as the nature of art and expression, the importance of
the imagination, and the relationship between executioner
and victim play in the novel.

I do this bit of suggestion about allegory to try to indicate the
double-edged nature of Nabokov's disclaimers about ways in
which his books can be read. It is possible that the need to dis-
claim is itself caused in part by Nabokov's realization that there
is support in his books for the approaches he disdains. The point
is that none of these approaches—the allegorical, the
satirical, the Freudian, the cultural, and so on—is basic to

3. See note 8 to Chapter Five.

the nature of the books he writes. None of them focuses what is fundamental to his fiction, though all of them may play some part, usually parodic. I have used *The Real Life of Sebastian Knight* as the occasion to suggest the modes which I believe generally subtend, as bract to flower, his fiction. They operate in *Invitation to a Beheading*, also. My purpose here, however, is to narrow the aperture, so to speak, and consider what happens in the book as a play, a staged drama which happens to appear, misleadingly, in the outward form of what one is used to call a "novel."

A remarkable number of instances in the book make this consideration plausible. The first speech the director of the prison makes to Cincinnatus is handled like a staged performance.

> "There is no ash tray here," he observed, gesturing with his cigarette; "oh well, let us drown it in what's left of the rest of this sauce . . . So. I would say the light is a bit harsh. Maybe if we . . . Oh, never mind; it will have to do."

The focus in this part of his act is on the condition of the stage: a property is missing, the lighting isn't correct. The passage continues:

> He unfolded the paper and, without putting on his horn-rimmed glasses, but holding them in front of his eyes, he began to read distinctly:
> "'Prisoner! In this solemn hour, when all eyes' . . . I think we had better stand," he interrupted himself with concern and rose from his chair. Cincinnatus also rose.
> "'Prisoner, in this solemn hour, when all eyes are upon thee. . . .'" (IB, 17)

The speech is planned, ceremonious. In Cincinnatus' recollection of the courtroom scene during which he received his judgment, he recalls details, such as the judges' makeup and the presence of a freshly painted park bench on which he left his fingerprints, which make the room seem part of a stage setting. Cincinnatus' impending execution is often spoken of as a "show"; the entire interview with his wife's family in Chapter 9 is a very badly managed stage scene complete with property men and a director; the very word *director*, when applied to the man in charge of the prison, becomes inseparable from suggestions of the director of a theatrical production.

Much is made especially of the presence of makeup and costumes. Cincinnatus wonders if "they will come to costume me" (IB,35) for the execution; the lawyer's face is made up with "dark blue eyebrows and long hairlip" (IB,37); Cincinnatus, expecting a visitor, "put on the best clothes he had with him . . . pulling on the white silk stockings which he, as a teacher, was entitled to wear at gala performances" (IB,79). The director, who wears various costumes in the course of the book, is described at one point this way: "Rodrig Ivanovich seemed even more spruce than usual: the dorsal part of his best frock coat was stuffed with cotton padding like a Russian coachman's, making his back look broad, smooth, and fat, his wig was glossy as new; the rich dough of his chin seemed to be powdered with flour, while in his buttonhole there was a pink waxy flower with a speckled moth" (IB,56). Sometimes— indeed, as often as not—the effect of this use of costumes and makeup is laughable, as for example when the director and M'sieur Pierre emerge from the tunnel they have dug to Cincinnatus' cell: "'It's us, it's us, it's us,' M'sieur Pierre finally managed with an effort, turning his chalk-white face to Cincinnatus, while his little yellow wig rose with a comic whistle and settled again" (IB,159). Moreover, the wearing of costumes affords a means for Nabokov to interchange the identities of characters at certain points: for instance, the scene in which Rodion leaves behind his leather apron and his red beard, which the director picks up, puts on and wears, thereby assuming the role of the jailer, and even going so far as to adopt his speech patterns and do his menial work.

59

Before this instance, however, in which costume change affords an easy means for the reader to understand how a change of identity can be accomplished, Nabokov has suggested shifting identities in a more mysterious way. In Chapter 3 what seems at first to be a somewhat confusing series of passages occurs.

> "Listen to him," chuckled the director. "He has to know everything. How do you like that, Roman Vissarionovich?"
>
> "Oh, my friend, you are so right," sighed the lawyer.
>
> "Yes, sir," continued the former, giving his keys a rattle. "You ought to be more cooperative, mister. All the time he's haughty, angry, snide. Last night I brought him some of them plums, you know, and what do you think? His excellency did not choose to eat them, his excellency was too proud. Yes sir! I started to tell you about that there new prisoner. You will have your fill of chit-chat with him. No need to mope as you do. Isn't that right, Roman Vissarionovich?"
>
> "That's right, Rodion, that's right," concurred the lawyer with an involuntary smile. (IB, 39)

At the beginning of this scene there have been three people present, Cincinnatus, the director, and Cincinnatus' lawyer. Suddenly Rodion, without introduction, speaks, and as suddenly the director, without any exit noted, disappears. This is intentional, in spite of the immediate effect of bewilderment, as the closing passages of the chapter make clear.

> Cincinnatus completed his trip around the terrace and returned to its south parapet. His eyes were making highly illegal excursions. Now he thought he distinguished that very bush in flower, that bird, that path disappearing under a canopy of ivy—
>
> "That will do now," said the director good-naturedly, tossing the broom in a corner and putting on again his frock coat. "Come along home."
>
> "Yes, it's time," responded the lawyer, looking at his watch.
>
> And the same little procession started back. In front was director Rodrig Ivanovitch, behind him lawyer Roman

> Vissarionovich, and behind him prisoner Cincinnatus, who
> after so much fresh air was beset by spasms of yawning. The
> back of the director's frock coat was soiled with chalk. (IB,44)

This last detail—the chalk on the director's back—suggests a
further interchangeability between characters. The lawyer has
appeared with chalk on the back of his coat on the previous
page. Hence, before change of costume has been introduced
to explain something of this sort, Nabokov has handled the in-
terchangeableness of three characters as though it were somehow in the nature of their beings.

This is done with other characters as well. At one point
Cincinnatus, and the reader with him, is led to expect a visit
from Marthe. As he thinks about his predicament, Cincinnatus says (in Chapter 5), "Tomorrow you will come" (IB, 60),
referring to Marthe. Later, the director says to Cincinnatus,
"Do not be crestfallen.... Tomorrow, tomorrow the thing
you dream of will become a reality" (IB, 70). As one learns still
later the director is thinking of M'sieur Pierre, but at this point
both Cincinnatus and the reader can take him to mean only
Marthe. This is carried as far as it can go, to M'sieur Pierre's
actual entrance into Cincinnatus' cell at the beginning of
Chapter 7. The point has been carefully made, however; one
is led to see Cincinnatus' wife and Cincinnatus' executioner
as, briefly but effectively, the same person.

A similar thing is done with Marthe's brothers. Cincinnatus
at one point imagines Marthe followed down the street by,
first, "a dark-mustachioed young blade" and then by a "fair-
haired fop." Later, in the frustrating visit Marthe's brood
makes to Cincinnatus, her twin brothers are described briefly
as "identical ... except that one had a golden mustache and
the other a pitch-black one" (IB,98). Again, as in the case of
Pierre and Marthe, the suggestion is a gentle but effective one:
Marthe's brothers are also her lovers. The accompanying

61

suggestion of incest is in perfect keeping with Marthe's sexual habits. She's a peachy chick.[4]

Finally, she is also associated closely with another character in the novel, the spider in Cincinnatus' cell. There are numerous spots where this suggestion is made,[5] but perhaps the most noticeable one occurs during a description of the cell: "The spider also moved. Up above, where the sloping window recess began, the well-nourished black beastie had found points of support for a first-rate web with the same resourcefulness as Marthe displayed when she would find, in what seemed the most unsuitable corner, a place and a method for hanging out laundry to dry" (IB, 119).

The recurrent theme of the interchangeability of identities seems to me commensurate with the suggestions made of the staged nature of life as it is led by all the characters in the novel, except Cincinnatus. If one is an actor, a marionette playing an assigned role, if one has no identity apart from that role, then it makes little difference how one's role is merged temporarily with the role of another, or how roles in general can be exchanged.[6]

Finally, two of M'sieur Pierre's appearances seem noteworthy in the context of costumes and makeup: "After dinner, quite formally, no longer in prison garb but in a velvet jacket, an arty bow tie and new, high-heeled, insinuatingly squeaking boots with glossy legs (making him somehow resemble an operatic woodman), M'sieur Pierre came in" (IB, 171), and "Rosy M'sieur Pierre, in a pea-green hunting habit, first inserted his head and then came in completely" (IB, 207).

4. I don't mean to be coy. See Cincinnatus' ill-timed entrance, p. 141.
5. Pages 13, 20, 32, 46, 66, 76, and 78.
6. One notices the similarity of this idea to Sebastian Knight's half brother's discovery at the end of his search. The use made of the "idea" in *Invitation to a Beheading*, however, is obviously in sharp contrast, a good instance showing Nabokov's relationship to his "material." See also the paragraph beginning "Let me put it this way" in *Strong Opinions* (147).

The suggestions of staged experience extend, as I have implied, into the very properties of Cincinnatus' environment. Rodion, for instance, seems at one point, "particularly proud of the fact that the spider was enthroned in a clean, impeccably correct web, which had been created, it was clear, just a moment before" (IB,78); at another juncture, "a summer thunderstorm, simply yet tastefully staged, was performed outside" (IB,129); and just before the tunnel diggers break through the wall into Cincinnatus' cell, "suddenly an extraordinary thing happened: some inner obstruction collapsed, and now the noises sounded with such vivid intensity (having in an instant made the transition from background to foreground, right up to the footlights) that their proximity was obvious" (IB,157).

There are even stage directions:

> A minute later, cooing politely, [the director] led in a diminutive Cecilia C., clad in a black raincoat. "I shall leave you two alone," he added benevolently, "even though it is against our rules, sometimes there are situations . . . exceptions . . . mother and son . . . I defer . . . "
> *Exit*, backing out like a courtier. (IB,130)

and, later:

> (Sighing) "Gone, gone . . . " (To the spider) "Enough, you've had enough . . . " (Showing his palm) "I don't have anything for you." (To Cincinnatus again) "It'll be dull, so dull without our little daughter . . . how she flitted about, what music she made, our spoiled darling, our golden flower." (Pause. Then, in a different tone) "What's the matter, good sir, why don't you ask those catchy questions any more?" (IB,171)

Within this world of makeup, costumes, interchangeable roles, footlights, properties and stage directions, various confrontations are handled at length in the way in which scenes in a stage play are handled. I have referred briefly to one of these, Marthe's visit, with her family, to Cincinnatus' cell. Others are worth looking at in more detail. First, Rodion's actions

63

after he has helped Cincinnatus down from the table on which he has been trying to look out of the barred window of his cell:

> Rodion, embracing him like a baby, carefully took him down, after which he moved the table with a violinlike sound to its previous place and sat on the edge, dangling the foot that was in the air, and bracing the other against the floor, having assumed the imitation-jaunty pose of operatic rakes in the tavern scene, while Cincinnatus picked at the sash of his dressing gown, and did his best not to cry.

This much goes no farther than most of the instances I have cited—it is little more than a comparison that gives some idea of what Rodion's position resembles. But in the next paragraph what has seemed to be a simple comparison is treated as though it were indeed the reality of the situation.

> Rodion was singing in his bass-baritone, rolling his eyes, brandishing the empty mug. Marthe used to sing that same dashing song once. Tears gushed from the eyes of Cincinnatus. On a climactic note Rodion sent the mug crashing against the floor and slid off the table. His song went on in chorus, even though he was alone. Suddenly he raised both arms and went out. (IB, 29–30)

This scene occurs in Chapter 2 and thus indicates early in the novel that the pervasive suggestions of staged performance that inform the novel are to be considered as more than a figurative means to imply something about the nature of the experience Cincinnatus is undergoing. It does this, of course, but Nabokov makes it do more. Cincinnatus' experience is not simply involved with people and activities that are *like* experience in a theater; he is involved with people and activities which *are* theater, whose nature is the nature of the experience of a stage play.

A second scene of this sort involves M'sieur Pierre's exertions with the chair in Cincinnatus' cell. It concludes, "Rodrig

Ivanovich, who had noticed nothing, was applauding wildly. The arena, however, remained empty. He cast a suspicious look at Cincinnatus, clapped some more, but without the former ardor, gave a little start and, in obvious distress, left the box. And thus the performance ended" (IB, 116). This is in part, as are the other scenes of its kind, entertainment for those who appreciate that sort of thing. What begins to become obvious as a number of such scenes accumulate is that Cincinnatus does not participate in them. Moreover, he observes such activity without the enthusiasm shown by, in this case, the director. In the scene cited before this one, in fact, what affords Rodion great pleasure causes Cincinnatus to weep. In the scene of M'sieur Pierre's agility with the chair, Cincinnatus' lack of approving response embarrasses, to some extent, the director; in the "suspicious look" he casts at Cincinnatus one sees, I think, a dramatization of precisely what Cincinnatus faces execution for, a failure to *be* what figures like Rodion, the director, and M'sieur Pierre are—a failure to be a stage puppet acting out a role.

Finally, in a third scene which has a similar effect, Cincinnatus confronts his mother, another marionette. He asks her, "'Why did you come? . . . I can see perfectly well that you are just as much of a parody as everybody and everything else. . . . You speak of candy! Why not 'goodies'? And why is your raincoat wet when your shoes are dry—see, that's careless. Tell the prop man for me'" (IB, 132). In this meeting one is given another example, more complex than those which have preceded it because of the appeal to Cincinnatus' filial sentiments, of the differences between Cincinnatus and the rest of the figures in the novel, and in this instance Nabokov suggests—again dramatically, concretely—why this difference can be the cause of Cincinnatus' being in his present position.

The performance toward which these accumulating scenes

65

are tending, and toward which the novel as a whole is tending, is, of course, Cincinnatus' execution. M'sieur Pierre announces the arrival of that auspicious occasion this way:

> "I found it, don't bother," said M'sieur Pierre, "so... the performance is scheduled for the day after tomorrow... In Thriller Square. Couldn't they have picked a better place... Remarkable!" (Goes on reading, muttering to himself) "Adults will be admitted... Circus subscription stubs will be honored... So, so, so... The performer of the execution, in red pantaloons... now this is nonsense—they've overdone it, as usual... " (To Cincinnatus) "Day after tomorrow, then. Did you understand—?" (IB, 176)

M'sieur Pierre, as a person who has no identity apart from the role he has been assigned in the stage production that is life to everyone but Cincinnatus, speaks of another man's execution as though it were also nothing but a performance. The presence of stage directions as part of the text is a gentle reminder of the identity of M'sieur Pierre as an actor in a play. Given this, it is easy to see why he is unfeeling, unaware, in fact, that death is a reality to Cincinnatus, not a performance in itself, or a part of a larger performance. This instance is as good as any in the novel to show how terrifying a mode Nabokov has invented through which to treat the effects on sensibility of the abandonment of one's human feeling and independence.

Through the various means, then, by which to suggest the experience of a stage play—costumes, makeup, shifting roles, property arrangement, sets, and scenes that are, and not metaphorically, theatrical—Nabokov makes the reader experience the novel in much the same way Cincinnatus experiences his life in the novel. It is, essentially, an attempt on the part of a group of actors to persuade an observer that the play they are performing is reality, an attempt to convince Cincinnatus that the values by which he has been judged are indispensable values, indeed the only values. In terms of the images

66

central to the "judgment" made on Cincinnatus, it is an attempt to prove to him that to be opaque (which is to say capable of keeping to one's self the secret that *is* one's self) in a world of transparencies (which is to say people who are thoroughly known, thoroughly predictable, capable of playing roles but not of living)—to be opaque in a world of transparencies is to commit a capital crime. The purport of the experience is, to put it too simply, that to be alive, to exercise judgment, choice, independence, and to imagine after one's needs, is a profoundly criminal act. The conflict in the novel, then, depends on the possibility that Cincinnatus will succumb to the pressure the actors are bringing to bear on him, and allow them to cut off his head. In order for such tension to work effectively, there must be as clear a dramatization of Cincinnatus' awareness of what is happening to him—or at least of his struggle to understand what is happening to him—as there is of the nature of the opposition. I have been focusing on the nature of the opposition. I want now to comment on the way Nabokov presents the protagonist.

Cincinnatus has to answer two questions during the course of the novel if he is to overcome the terms of the drama in which his adversaries are attempting to include him. First, he must discover where the play is being performed, and who the real director of the performance is. Second, he must find out what, if anything, can be done to change the situation. He answers both these questions during the course of the book, but only with great labor, of which his attempts to express himself serve as emblems. The movement to answer these questions is the means by which Cincinnatus' change is achieved, the means by which the meaning of the experience the novel presents is defined. I will deal with this movement in two ways, a brief and suggestive one first, and then a more complex and detailed one.

One way of getting at this movement is to consider the top-

67

ographical situation Cincinnatus is in at the novel's opening, and the one he stays in until its end—to consider, simply, *where* he is: in prison. How is his imprisonment defined? What does it mean that he is in prison for almost the duration of the book?

Nabokov suggests (almost immediately) the direction to take in answering this question. In Chapter 1 there is a sudden reversal of the roles of jailer and prisoner. The director ends his first solemn speech to Cincinnatus by saying, "That will be all. I shall not keep you any longer. Let me know if you should need anything" (IB,18). Instead of leaving Cincinnatus in his cell at this point, which is what one would expect, the director "sat down at the table and began to write rapidly, thus indicating that the audience was over. Cincinnatus went out" (IB,18). He walks through various corridors, emerges from the fortress, walks to the city, along its streets, and finally arrives at his own house. Free, or so it seems. But then, "Cincinnatus ran up the front steps, pushed open the door, and entered his lighted cell. He turned around, but already he was locked in" (IB,20). This is *not* an hallucination indicating Cincinnatus' desire to escape his cell and the concomitant impossibility of his doing it. It begins the series of suggestions that Cincinnatus is his own cell, and that no matter where he goes he is in it. Nabokov develops this carefully.

Early in the next chapter this passage appears as part of an account of Cincinnatus' past: "In the course of time the safe places became ever fewer: the solicitous sunshine of public concern penetrated everywhere, and the peephole in the door was placed in such a way that in the whole cell there was not a single point that the observer on the other side of the door could not pierce with his gaze" (IB,24–25). This refers to Cincinnatus' youth, yet it is written in such a way that it seems to concern his present situation. The effect is to continue the suggestion that he has always been in his present situation.

This is suggested again immediately, in a different way, by the juxtaposition of paragraphs.

> Then Cincinnatus put on the black dressing gown . . . the black slippers with pompoms, and the black skullcap, and began walking about the cell, as he had done every morning since the first day of his confinement.
>   Childhood on suburban lawns. They played ball, pig, daddy-long-legs. . . . (IB,25)

The placement of the end sentence of the one paragraph and the beginning sentence of the next serves the same purpose as the passage I have previously quoted: to suggest that Cincinnatus has been in his cell since an early age.

As these suggestions continue they are modulated. Cincinnatus is described after his bath: "He was very thin, and now, as the light of the setting sun exaggerated the shadows of his ribs, the very structure of his rib cage seemed a triumph of cryptic coloration inasmuch as it expressed the barred nature of his surroundings, of his gaol" (IB,65). It isn't only a matter any longer of his being placed in a cell because he is essentially different from everyone else; the idea that his body is his jail begins to play in the conception, too. The two suggestions are brought together in a later passage: "His gaolers, who in fact were everyone, seemed more tractable; in the confining phenomena of life his reason sought out a possible trail" (IB,73).

The passages I have cited thus far are all spoken by the narrator about Cincinnatus; as such they tell something about the nature of his confinement that he himself does not know. As the novel continues, however, the voice that utters these ideas becomes that of Cincinnatus himself. In Chapter 8, Cincinnatus tries again to write something about his experience. He begins, "Today is the eighth day . . . and [I am] still alive, that is, the sphere of my own self still limits and eclipses my being" (IB,89); continues, "I am here through an error—not in this prison specifically—but in this whole terrible, striped world" (IB,91); and concludes, "The horrible 'here,' the dark dungeon, in which a relentlessly howling heart is encarcerated, this 'here' holds and constricts me" (IB,93). Cincinnatus himself considers his imprisonment as something more basic than simply being in a cell made of stone and iron; he associates his cell specifically with his self, the world, and time. This is an immensely important discovery to him, something Nabokov through the narrator has made the reader aware of from the beginning of the novel but something it takes Cincinnatus time and effort to understand. But he does understand it, and in understanding it arrives at the terms through which he can answer the first question, what is the nature of the drama that is being staged for me with its chief aim being my inclusion in it? His prison, where he awaits execution, is, essentially, his own self, the world in which that self exists, and time. Thus the task becomes, seen from this perspective, to extricate himself from this prison, to free his being from his self, his world, and from time.

To consider the situation Cincinnatus is in, then—to look simply at the way in which his prison is treated—is one way to get some idea of the movement that is basic to the novel. I have handled this separately to give some idea of the movement in connection with a fairly simple (for Nabokov) notion. The use of the cell that Nabokov makes is, however simple, central to the novel, and contains the essential implication of its meaning: that as Cincinnatus' cell is himself before it is anything else, so the drama that threatens to include his beheading is of his own making—he is the director of it as well as its potential victim.

The distinction that Cincinnatus makes between his "being" and "self" is crucial to the novel. His being is more basic than his self; the presence of the staged experience that Cincinnatus is confronted with affords terms by which one can understand this distinction without having to rely on the more abstruse terms, *being* and *self*, completely. The novel asks one to consider the self as a mode through which a person's being realizes and expresses itself. The self is a role the being plays. Given this set of terms, or this metaphorical perspective, one can accept the credibility of change, the possibility that Cincinnatus can indeed alter his situation. The self that is a prison cell has been formed in a certain way, specifically in the manner that the world it finds itself in is formed. Hence the danger to Cincinnatus' being, that opaqueness which no one else in the novel has. If he allows the prison-cell self—that is, the self that accepts the guilty verdict and awaits the execution—to remain unchanged, he is playing the role his "here" asks him to play. What he must do to escape his cell is to create another self through which to express his being, a self more in keeping with the opacity which is unique to him. How foolish it is, after all, for an opaque being to present himself as transparent. The stage of the play is, then, Cincinnatus' mind; what must be changed is the way he imagines his role and the roles of others in the world he lives in. Whereas with the other characters in the novel any role will do—there can be the interchanging of roles I have discussed earlier—with Cincinnatus there is a wrong role and a right one. He is playing the wrong one at the novel's beginning; the experience of the book is his search for the right one. And only he can do this without disappearing, precisely because he is opaque; he has a being, something more real than a performing self.

The imagination, so important in *Sebastian Knight*, is the means by which Cincinnatus can change his self. As such, it is the most pervasive theme in the novel, the thread which is interwoven with the most subtlety and completeness, and is difficult to talk about. Rather than discuss this theme chronologically, in accord with the progress of the narration, I will approach it through the aspects of Cincinnatus' imagination itself.

First, consider the clarity with which Cincinnatus sees the nature of the people around him, from a point very early in the book. He has no real problem here; the recognition of the insubstantialness of everyone else is relatively simple. I have quoted the passage in which he calls his mother a parody; at various places in the first seventy pages of the novel he calls other characters, particularly the director, such things as "specters, werewolves, parodies" (IB, 40) and "rag doll, coachman, painted swine" (IB, 57). A focal instance of his recognition occurs on page seventy: "For thirty years I have lived among specters that appear solid to the touch, concealing from them the fact that I am alive and real—but now that I have been caught, there is no reason to be constrained with you. At least I shall test for myself all the unsubstantiality of this world of yours." In another passage involving this same clear recognition, however, he reveals the problems that really trouble him. He speaks to his lawyer.

> I want to share with you some conclusions I have reached. I am surrounded by some sort of wretched specters, not by people. They torment me as can torment only senseless visions, bad dreams, dregs of delirium, the drivel of nightmares and everything that passes down here for real life. In theory one would wish to wake up. But wake up I cannot without outside help, and yet I fear this help terribly, and my very soul has grown lazy and accustomed to its snug swaddling clothes. Of all the specters that surround me, you, Roman Vissarionovich, are probably the most wretched, but on the other hand—in view of your logical position in our invented habitus—you are in a manner of speaking, an adviser, a defender. (IB, 36)

If it is relatively easy for Cincinnatus to see that those around him are insubstantial specters in an invented world, it is much harder for him to want to change it, much less know how to.

This last speech indicates two things which hamper Cincinnatus: his fear of waking up from the invention that is so wretched, and, more basic than this fear, his laziness. The invented world of specters has, after all, always been his world, and the habit of this invention is immensely, indescribably difficult to overcome.

My second focus is, in fact, the habitual imagination, the acceptance of a way of seeing things, the acceptance of things themselves as one has been taught to see them. This, coupled with the fear of what one might find instead if he changed his mind, and the fear of the effort needed to change anything in the first place, is the source of Cincinnatus' problems. In his first attempt to write down the secret of his existence he confronts this:

> I still ought to record, to leave something. I am not an ordinary—I am the one among you who is alive—Not only are my eyes different, and my hearing, and my sense of taste... but most important, I have the capacity to conjoin all this in one point... but here is what I want to express: between his movement and the movement of the laggard shadow—that second, that syncope—there is the rare kind of time in which I live—the pause, the hiatus, when the heart is like a feather.... But how can I write of this when I am afraid of not having time to finish and of stirring up all these thoughts in vain?... I'm wrong when I keep repeating that there is no refuge in the world for me. There is! I'll find it! ... This is unhealthy, though—what am I doing: as it is I am weak, and here I am exciting myself, squandering the last of my strength. What anguish, oh what anguish... And it is obvious to me that I have not yet removed the final film from my fear. (IB, 52–53)

When he tries to write the second time he comes back to these same themes: the necessity to peel away layers of habitual thought and to remove his fear of doing this, of waking up. This passage, again, comes from the early part of the book; though Cincinnatus is conscious of his fear he is rather help-

73

less before it. Much later, in Chapter 19, the tone has changed markedly—he is calmer, more reasoning.

> "Everything has fallen into place," he wrote, "that is, everything has duped me—all of this theatrical, pathetic stuff—the promises of a volatile maiden, a mother's moist gaze, the knocking on the wall, a neighbor's friendliness, and, finally, those hills which broke out in a deadly rash. Everything has duped me as it fell into place, everything. This is the dead end of this life, and I should not have sought salvation within its confines. It is strange that I should have sought salvation. (IB, 205)

This is the Cincinnatus who is very close to his final, liberating gesture with which the novel ends, seeing himself duped because he has accepted the drama habitual imagination conceived in the terms it was taught to conceive. This is, of course, dangerous, "the dead end of life," and the danger is not a figurative danger at all but a literal one; to accept from someone else the terms by which life might be understood is, simply, to be executed, to lose one's head. The particular mode of execution that Nabokov chose for this book is integral to its basic purport.

The passage that expresses most terrifyingly this danger occurs as Cincinnatus lies in the dark of his cell, summarizing the events of his two weeks in the fortress. It is a lengthy passage (IB, 155–56) and closes with a chilling *danse macabre*, a vision of what happens when a man does not imagine for himself:

> And now, emerging from the darkness, the lighted figures joined hands and formed a ring—and, slightly swaying to one side, lurching, lagging, they began a circling movement, which at first was stiff and dragging, but then gradually became more even, free and rapid, and now they were whirling in earnest, and the monstrous shadow of their shoulders and heads passed and repassed ever more quickly across the stone vaults, and the inevitable joker who, when whirling in a reel, kicks his legs

> high, to amuse his more prim companions, cast on the walls
> the huge black zigzag of his hideous prance. (IB, 156)

The whole passage focuses the dependence of everyone in the
novel, as well as the whole charade of life the novel presents,
in the mind of Cincinnatus, who "allowed them the right to
exist, supported them, nourished them with himself," who
yielded to "the temptation of logical development."

Given these two steps, then—Cincinnatus' realization that
the people around him are specters and should be "tested" (as
he puts it) out of existence, and his own habituation to this
spectral existence and his fear of exerting the effort to change
it—given this, what is the alternative? What can the imagination replace these insubstantial parodies with?

The novel offers various suggestions in answer to these questions. Early on Cincinnatus stops in the hall of the prison and
has a vision. As he imagines the city emanating from himself,
it is transformed from the dead thing it really is into something
pulsing with unusual life. What is important here, in addition
to the exercise of imagination in a way that is not conditioned
by the charade of his experience, is that Cincinnatus still uses
the objects with which he is familiar as the substance of what
he imagines. This is, in short, a beginning stage in his process
of freeing his imagination from the bonds he has so long im-
posed upon it. Since it is a beginning stage, it is not possible
that he can as yet totally disengage himself from the details of
his life; the change consists in his rearranging them.

This is developed further in a later passage, as Cincinnatus
tries for the second time to write down the essence of his experience.

> But what gleams shine through at night, and what—. It exists,
> my dream world, it must exist, since, surely there must be an
> original of the clumsy copy. Dreamy, round, and blue, it turns
> slowly toward me. It is as if you are lying supine, with eyes
> closed, on an overcast day, and suddenly the gleam stirs under

your eyelids, and slowly becomes first a langorous smile, then a warm feeling of contentment, and you know that the sun has come out from behind the clouds. With just such a feeling my world begins: the misty air gradually clears, and it is suffused with such radiant, tremulous kindness, and my soul expanses so freely in its native realm. (IB,93–94)

The details which follow are the details of the world Cincinnatus has always known—it seems impossible to escape them—and again there is a sense of their rearrangement. What is added is the change of mode in which these details and rearrangements are presented. In the first instance Cincinnatus had a vision the narrator reported; in this instance Cincinnatus is writing, thinking, speaking in his own voice. And he is theorizing about imagination while he is imagining. The dimension of self-consciousness has been added; he verbalizes and in this way makes articulate what has before been purely visual. The real world, which is the world Cincinnatus dreams of, is reproduced and reflected as the world of staged experience that is being played before him. As his remarks make clear, finally, the parody is a wretched reversal of the kind of experience he dreams of.

There is a reality, then, beyond the one performed by the director and Rodion and Marthe and the rest of the specters of Cincinnatus' present prison, a world he is groping to attain. In Chapter 10, the symmetrical center both of the narrative and of the time span Cincinnatus' experience covers, it becomes clear to him that the way to this world is the path of imagination.

"Ten days have passed like this, and I haven't gone crazy. And then, of course, there is always some hope... Indistinct, as if under water, but therefore all the more attractive. You speak of escape... I think, I surmise, that there is someone else too who is concerned with it... Certain hints... But what if this is only a deception, a fold in the fabric mimicking a human face..."
He sighed and paused.

"This is curious," said M'sieur Pierre. "What are these hopes, and who is this savior?"

"Imagination," replied Cincinnatus. (IB, 114)

The problem, then, has become not only realizing that his current worlds is spectral, that the way out of it is to imagine a different world, and that the effort of doing so is almost superhuman, involving as it does the removal of habitual imaginative patterns as well as the fear of doing so; it has come to include also the need, caused by the power of habit and fear, of some outside help. Cincinnatus can't get this outside help from any person in the prison of his self. But there are two incidents that indicate there is a kind of outside help which is available, and which he can trust.

I am thinking of the incidents involving the acorn and the moth, the former tied in with the novel *Quercus*, part of which Cincinnatus reads in his cell. *Quercus'* importance consists, first of all, in the fact that it is imaginative literature through which Cincinnatus becomes aware of the power of imagination. "It seemed as though the author were sitting with his camera somewhere among the topmost branches of the Quercus, spying out and catching his prey" (IB, 123) the narrator tells us, suggesting what Cincinnatus is made to imagine by reading the book. The author of the novel is controlling time, and, most important, he looks down upon his subjects as though they were *his* prey. This is "outside help." It is further valuable because it gives Cincinnatus a new perspective on his death. "Or else he would begin imagining how the author, still a young man, living, so they said, on an island in the North Sea—would be dying himself; and it was funny because the only real, genuinely unquestionable thing here was only death itself, the inevitability of the author's physical death" (IB, 123–24). This is a real death Cincinnatus is made to imagine, not one that is the final performance in a series of performances by a bunch of specters and parodies. The basic value

77

of Cincinnatus' reading this novel is, it seems to me, that he is led to imagine from another perspective. It is also important that the perspective is associated with an organic, natural object—an oak tree—as though there is something in its nature that is not present in the specters which surround him.

In light of the experience Cincinnatus has while reading this book, consider this passage:

> Cincinnatus undressed and got in bed with *Quercus*. The author was already getting to the civilized ages, to judge by the conversation of three merry wayfarers, Tit, Pud, and the Wandering Jew who were taking swigs of wine from their flasks on the cool moss beneath the black vespertine oak.
>
> "Will no one save me?" Cincinnatus suddenly asked aloud and sat up on the bed (opening his pauper's hands, showing that he had nothing).
>
> "Can it be that no one will?" repeated Cincinnatus, gazing at the implacable yellowness of the walls and still holding up his empty palms.
>
> The draft became a leafy breeze. From the dense shadows above there fell and bounced on the blanket a large dummy acorn, twice as large as life, splendidly painted a glossy buff, and fitting its cork cup as snugly as an egg. (IB, 125–26)

The moth is also organic and natural, as well as an ancient symbol for the transformed soul.[7] It gets away from the jailer before he can feed it to the spider: "Its flight, swooping and lumbering, lasted only a short time. Rodion picked up the towel and, swinging wildly, attempted to knock down the blind flyer; but suddenly it disappeared as if the very air had swallowed it" (IB, 204). Rodion can't find it—he doesn't have the necessary imagination—but "Cincinnatus . . . had seen perfectly well where the moth had settled" (IB, 204). The moth seems to disappear in much the same way Cincinnatus has

7. Speaking of painters who have used the butterfly in their work, Nabokov once said, "That in some cases the butterfly symbolizes something (e.g. Psyche) lies utterly outside my area of interest" (SO, 168).

been described as seeming to disappear (on page 121); again, there is a suggestion of outside help. There are two other striking passages in the novel which I would like to look at in the context of "outside help." The first of these passages describes the childhood experience Cincinnatus remembers, his walking on air. The description draws together much that is central to the book. The context of the memory is Cincinnatus' statement that "Life has worn me down"; the memory itself is associated with the first understanding that "things which to me had seemed natural were actually forbidden" and with Cincinnatus' first attempt to write—as he says, "I must have just learned how to make letters." He is set apart from the other children, watching them play from a window above them (perhaps as the writer of *Quercus* watches the activity beneath him, controlling it). He is suddenly driven "within myself" by the oppression of the games being played on the school yard—he tries "to slow down and slip out of the senseless life that was carrying me onward." As he begins to do this a figure of authority, the "senior educator," appears at the end of the corridor, flourishing his towel. At this point, "unconsciously and innocently," Cincinnatus steps onto the elastic air, successfully, and part of the effect is similar to the effect he achieves at the end of the novel: "I saw below me, like pale daisies, the upturned faces of the stupified children, and the pedagoguette, who seemed to be falling backward." The account ends as Rodion turns out the light Cincinnatus is writing by.

This is a memory of the one time Cincinnatus, as a child, exercised publicly his own imagination. The memory of this occurs as he writes in his cell, and though it isn't really help from the outside physically, it is help from the past. He has done before what it is necessary that he do now; it is important that the action is incompletely remembered, for the total effect of doing what he has once begun and must do again has to wait for its present attempt.

One other point here. Cincinnatus' memory of this incident seems to me stimulated by one of the characters. He has met little Emmie on a window seat, and has asked her, "Won't you please take me out there?" As soon as this is uttered Rodion appears down the corridor to take Cincinnatus back to his cell. Part of Emmie's importance in the novel is suggested here; she is a child, albeit a corrupted child who accepts the system and the play she is engaged in. But she is a child and certain enthusiasms and eccentricities, such as her drawings in Cincinnatus' book, her bouncing of the ball, her trapeze act in Cincinnatus' cell, are tolerated. She affords Cincinnatus a glimpse of childhood, especially in the window seat scene, that scene acting as an impetus, I think, for Cincinnatus' later memory of having exercised his imagination once, as a child.

The second important and striking scene of this kind is Cecilia C.'s description of the *nonnons* in Chapter 12. The *nonnons*—notnots—are jumbled objects that are rearranged into recognizable objects by a jumbled mirror. They are, as Cecilia C. says, "marvelous gimmicks," games for one's amusement. What happens as Cecilia C. describes them, however, is that she is led to go beyond their gamelike quality to a different kind of consideration: "Oh, I remember what fun it was, and how it was a little frightening—what if suddenly nothing should come out?—to pick up a new, incomprehensible *nonnon* and bring it near the mirror, and see your hand get all scrambled, and at the same time see the meaningless *nonnon* turn into a charming picture" (IB, 136). I take this to be an emblem of Cincinnatus' experience: his criminality consists of his messing up the nice game of *nonnons* played by all the transparent people; he jumbles them, renders them meaningless—or is capable of this—and must be destroyed. There is more to it than this, but I think that is the direction one goes in in connection with the *nonnons*. What is clearer is Cincinnatus' reaction to Cecilia C.'s brief account of the game:

> He suddenly noticed the expression in Cecilia C.'s eyes—just for an instant, an instant—but it was as if something real, unquestionable (in this world, where everything was subject to question), had passed through, as if a corner of this horrible life had curled up, and there was a glimpse of the lining. In his mother's gaze, Cincinnatus suddenly saw that ultimate, secure, all-explaining and from-all-protecting spark that he knew how to discern in himself also. What was this spark so piercingly expressing now? It does not matter what—call it horror, or pity ... But rather let us say this: the spark proclaimed such a tumult of truth that Cincinnatus's soul could not help leaping for joy. The instant flashed and was gone. (IB, 136)

Here the help is from outside, inadvertently from a specter, and Cincinnatus gets another glimpse of the possibility that eventually saves him. [8]

What is the situation, then? A man recognizes the wretched spectral nature of his invented world, recognizes that to escape it he must imagine another sort of world altogether, yet fears to do this and is so habituated to his present invention that to change it seems to involve more effort than he is capable of, tries therefore to find outside help, yet knows none of the specters can be trusted to give it to him, receives instead outside help of another kind from a book and a moth, a memory of

---

8. The most basic outside help is the narrator, peeking occasionally through a fold in the fabric. The narrator of *Invitation to a Beheading* is, of course, closer to being Nabokov himself than are the narrators of most of his other novels, especially those in the first person. This narrator drops acorns, "teaches" Cincinnatus by saying things for him that he learns later to say for himself, calls attention to the fact of the composition, and is generally on Cincinnatus' side. Moreover, to distinguish, as I am implicitly doing, between stage play and narrative—between *what* is presented, that is, and the *voice* that presents—is to emphasize the connection between Cincinnatus and the narrator. The narrative itself becomes, in this light, the mode of escape from the play. It is tempting to take another step (as the scaffolding crumbles) and consider an analogy: as Cincinnatus escapes the play through the narrative, so the author escapes the book, to which Cincinnatus is eternally confined; the author's perspective on his novel is as Cincinnatus' perspective on his play. Another paradigm.

childhood and a reminiscence of his mother's. Yet his problems remain, because he remains. What can be done with the suggestions the acorn and the moth have brought him? Even after they appear he stays in his cell, which is to say remains constricted by the limits of his present self.

What he can do, simply, is use his pencil. In regard to the theme of the use of imagination in *Beheading* the locus of the idea is, as the pages devoted to *Quercus* imply, the power of the word. This is suggested first by certain stylistic quirks Nabokov works into the narrative. In the following passage the director speaks first:

> "Having learned from trustworthy sources that your fate has been sort of sealed," he began in a fruity bass, "I have deemed it my duty, dear sir . . ."
> Cincinnatus said: "Kind. You. Very." (This still had to be arranged.)
> "You are very kind," said an additional Cincinnatus, having cleared his throat. (IB, 15)

In the next one the lawyer makes an absent-minded remark: "'Oh thanks, don't worry about it, it's nothing.' . . . And with his eyes he literally scoured the corners of the cell. It was plain that he was upset by the loss of that precious object. It was plain. The loss of the object upset him. The object was precious. He was upset by the loss of the object" (IB, 35–36). In both instances, first with the arrangement of words into a sentence, then with the play with the arrangement of sentences, one is made aware that something is in the process of being written—one is given an emblem of the imagination at work, with words, reminded of the infinite possibility of word combinations, and of the necessity of choice in the imaginative process.[9] This is, of course, a game, but it is made to serve a

9. This particular kind of notation will recur in the succeeding chapters, though I will modulate the format somewhat. In addition to the various instances that follow, note the shift from textbook French to stereotyped Western lingo and back to French

more significant purpose, which becomes clear later while Cincinnatus is himself trying to write. In this case, as in others I have mentioned, there is a transference from the narrator's voice to Cincinnatus'. Two segments of Cincinnatus' "diary" are relevant here:

> Not knowing how to write, but sensing with my criminal intuition how words are combined, what one must do for a commonplace word to come alive and to share its neighbor's sheen, heat, shadow, while reflecting itself in its neighbor and renewing the neighboring word in the process, so that the whole line is live iridescence; while I sense the nature of this kind of word propinquity, I am nevertheless unable to achieve it, yet that is what is indispensable to me for my task, a task of not now and not here. (IB,93)

Why the iridescent combination of words is "indispensable to my task," a segment which follows a page later tells us: "There is in the world not a single human being who can speak my language; or, more simply, not a single human who can speak; or even more simply, not a single human" (IB,95). The ability to speak, to put words together so that language lives and renews itself, becomes, then, a definition of "human," and one realizes clearly how important it is to Cincinnatus, as he tries to free himself of the terms of other people's imaginations, to teach himself to write. His pencil, then, *is his way out*, and the entries he makes for his "diary" are the most important actions he participates in during the novel. It is through them that he learns to free himself. Very early in the novel, moreover, there appears, in italics, the idea on which the existence of the transparent judges of Cincinnatus is based.

> Those around him understood each other at the first word, since they had no words that would end in an unexpected way, perhaps in some archaic letter, an upsilamba, becoming a bird

---

(our deviously "forgetful" author) in *Bend Sinister* (37), and the narrator's directions to himself in the same novel (107–108).

> or a catapult with wondrous consequences. In the dusty little
> museum on Second Boulevard, where they used to take him as
> a child, and where he himself would later take his charges,
> there was a collection of rare, marvelous objects, but all the
> townsmen except Cincinnatus found them just as limited and
> transparent as they did each other. *That which does not have a*
> *name does not exist.* Unfortunately, everything had a name.
> (IB, 26)

That which does not have a name does not exist. In that idea
resides the answer to all of Cincinnatus' problems, for if something needs a name to exist, all one has to do to make it cease
existing is to take its name away. This is precisely what happens at the end of the novel, when everything that has been
inimical to Cincinnatus disintegrates.

The last chapter opens as Cincinnatus is being led to his
execution. This paragraph focuses the many suggestions I have
been trying to put together.

> Throughout this whole journey Cincinnatus was busy trying to
> cope with his choking, wrenching, implacable fear. He realized
> that this fear was dragging him precisely into that false logic of
> things that had gradually developed around him, but from
> which he had still somehow been able to escape that morning.
> The very thought that this chubby, red-cheeked hunter was
> going to hack at him was already an inadmissable sickening
> weakness, drawing Cincinnatus into a system that was perilous
> to him. He fully understood all this, but like a man unable to
> resist arguing with a hallucination, even though he knows per-
> fectly well that the entire masquerade is staged in his own
> brain, Cincinnatus tried in vain to out-wrangle his fear, despite
> his understanding that he ought actually to rejoice at the awak-
> ening whose proximity was presaged by barely noticeable
> phenomena. (IB, 213)

It is very much like Nabokov to turn the key of a novel in a
simile, to insert it almost as an afterthought, as he does here:
"like a man unable to resist arguing with a hallucination, even
though he knows perfectly well that the entire masquerade is

staged in his own brain." The last step in the process of Cincinnatus' freeing himself of the stage play that has threatened
to annihilate him is suggested by his repeated assertion at key
moments in the mounting of the scaffold, "By myself." It is
finally, after great labor, an assertion of independence, and
once it is made, once Cincinnatus dissociates himself from the
charade, it must of necessity crumble as it does, for it no
longer is able to nourish itself on Cincinnatus. He has, simply,
changed his mind and, as a result, not lost his head.

Nabokov labels *Invitation to a Beheading* accurately, I
think, when he calls it "a violin in a void"; and yet what the
book suggests in its own peculiar way is that the small, transient strain of that violin is of more permanent value than the
context in which it sounds. *Beheading* is also a shimmering instance of the inappropriateness of much critical aspersion of
Nabokov's supposed morbidity and his alleged fascination with
denizens of the psychological netherworld. Its bright presence
helps one see how various and inclusive his fictional universe
is. The tone is light, and the "hero" drops his quotation marks,
slays his dragon, and departs a gruesome world for an incom-
parably preferable one. Even if one considers the novel a
paradigm of the value of parody to Nabokov as a novelist—the
humorous dismissal of fictional modes of perception that presume to substitute themselves for life—it is still a trope for
triumph. It is that and a good deal else—a comedy, finally, as
The Tempest is a comedy, and as *Bend Sinister* is not.[10]

---

10. I have made several allusive connections between *Invitation to a Beheading*
and *Bend Sinister*. Nabokov has spoken of these two novels as "the two bookends of
grotesque design between which my other volumes tightly huddle" (SO,287). In the
same place he labeled "first-rate" Stanley Edgar Hyman's essay "The Handle: *Invitation to a Beheading* and *Bend Sinister*," which appeared in Alfred Appel, Jr., and
Charles Newman (eds.), *Nabokov: Criticism, Reminiscences, Translations and Trib-
utes* (Evanston: Northwestern University Press, 1970), 60–71.

FOUR

Laughter in the Dark: The Novel as Film

I MOVING PICTURES

The structure of almost all of Vladimir Nabokov's longer works of fiction (the *possible* exception is *The Eye*) is dependent on the use of modes of artistic perception not usually associated with the form we traditionally label "the novel." In *Invitation to a Beheading*, as I have just argued, he employs certain tactics of staged drama to embody the spectral voices seeking Cincinnatus' allegiance and death (and to distinguish them from the narrative voice which encourages him to live); *Pale Fire* volleys the reader's expectations against a backboard of the familiar apparatus of formal scholarship; *The Gift* responds structurally to the demands of both a literary history and a biography, the latter of which also informs *Pnin*.[1] Sometimes (*e.g., The Real Life of Sebastian Knight, Despair*) the form of a particular kind of "novel" (*e.g.,* the detective story and the "double" story,[2] respectively) is employed for purposes other than, and beyond, those for which it is normally in-

1. See Chapter Six.
2. See Chapter Five.

tended. The effect—and, because of the consistency with which Nabokov employs the technique, I would guess the intention—of this is, broadly speaking, at least twofold: continually to remind the reader, through the form of the book that he is reading, that he is reading a book, and to embed in the form of the book itself the possibilities of parody that are more immediately obvious in particular details, character gestures, and diction. In terms of the conception of fiction as a literary mode, the major implication of the use of this technique is that one can see fiction as nothing else but parody, regardless of how intensely the writer seems to be concerned with verisimilitude. Thus, from this perspective, a work—say *Germinal*, or *Sister Carrie*, for instance—of the most obvious "naturalistic" intentions is no less a parody than *Lolita*, a parody, of course, of the life it tries to reproduce. One implication (among others) that I find central to Nabokov's fiction is that, since any fiction is a parody of life, the best fiction, or the fiction that is most consciously itself, is the fiction that acknowledges as completely as it can be made to do its own parodic nature. To put this in terms which have traditionally riddled commentaries on fiction, the last thing a writer should try to do is bamboozle his readers into "identifying with," or "sympathizing with," his characters. The object, on the contrary, is to keep the reader at a substantial distance from not only the characters but the book in which they appear, to put him as much as possible in the place where he competes with the author, to give him a sense of participating in the game of composition, to remind him, in short, of the nature of the experience he is involved in; that is, reading, confronting an imaginative creation that has its own principles of reality that do not ask to be viewed from the same perspective one takes on other aspects of his life. [3] It may be, in fact, that this effect of

3. Nabokov has been explicit about this in interviews with Herbert Gold (SO,95): "My characters are galley slaves"; and Alfred Appel, Jr. (SO,72): "I think that what I

forcing the reader into considering life from an unfamiliar point of view is part of the cause of what seems to be a widespread resistance to his work. As he has said, "There are people whom parody upsets."[4]

Whatever the theoretical directions one tries to follow, the presence of the technique is pervasive. And the most frequent mode of artistic perception Nabokov employs by means of which to structure his "novels" is the motion picture;[5] it shows up in *King, Queen, Knave* and *Lolita* particularly, but in both those books, as in others where it is less insistent, it coexists with other modes. The novel whose structure, and meaning, depends most pervasively on the motion picture as a form through which the experience of the book is to be perceived and evaluated is *Laughter in the Dark*.

Even a casual reading of *Laughter in the Dark* reveals that motion pictures play a central part in the novel, at least as far as the characters themselves are interested in them. Margot Peters dreams from her adolescence in her family's squalid tenement of becoming a film star; after she has set up shop on her own she tries, on the strength of bravura alone, to make connections with a producer. She meets Albinus while she is working as an usher in a movie house, and once she has hooked him she persuades him to finance a picture in which she has the second female lead, a picture which is produced and the reader views in Chapter 23. Moreover, Axel Rex has

---

would welcome at the close of a book of mine is a sensation of its world receding in the distance and stopping somewhere there suspended afar like a picture in a picture"; and in various places in *Speak, Memory*, of which the following is representative: "It should be understood that competition in chess problems is not really between Black and White but between the composer and hypothetical solver (just as in a first-rate work of fiction the real clash is not between the characters but between the author and the world)" (SM, 290). He subsequently altered his identification of the combatants to "the author and the reader" (SO, 183). See also note 21 below.

4. Appel interview (SO, 77).

5. The only things more recurrent in his fiction are butterflies (with the accompanying suggestion that human life may be instaric) and chess. See note 19 below.

spent some of his devious artistic energy making cartoons, and it is he whom Albinus requests to consider helping animate certain paintings by old masters. In fact, the novel opens with this idea: "It had to do with colored animated drawings. . . . How fascinating it would be, he [Albinus] thought, if one could use this method for having some well-known picture . . . perfectly reproduced on the screen in vivid colors and then brought to life—movement and gesture graphically developed in complete harmony with their static state in the picture . . . little by little bringing the figures and the light into the [original] order, settling them down, so to speak, and ending it all with the first picture."[6] Albinus broaches the idea to Rex, but apparently, as the novel progresses, drops it and has to settle for his part in the production of the miserable film in which Margot has a role.

This surface concern is so presented, however, that very soon one becomes aware that much more is at stake, that Albinus' idea, Rex's possible collaboration in its fulfillment, and Margot's having a part in a movie are all determining factors in a pattern that involves their total experience with each other, not just their superficial interest in the cinema.

That the mode of the telling of the story is more important than the salient events of the story is focused in the first two paragraphs of Chapter 1.

> Once upon a time there lived in Berlin, Germany, a man called Albinus. He was rich, respectable, happy; one day he abandoned his wife for the sake of a youthful mistress; he loved; was not loved; and his life ended in disaster.
>
> This is the whole of the story and we might have left it at that had there not been profit and pleasure in the telling; and although there is plenty of space on a gravestone to contain, bound in moss, the abridged version of a man's life, detail is always welcome.

6. *Laughter in the Dark* (New York: New Directions, 1960), 8–9. All further quotations are from this edition and are noted in parentheses following the passages.

The next five paragraphs (through page 11) are given to the development of Albinus' idea of the animation of paintings by
old masters, thus keying the form in which "welcome detail" is
to be presented; it will be animated still life, or motion picture,
and the paragraph in which Albinus seems to relinquish his
idea is intended rather to signal the transmutation of that idea
into the structural principle on which the rest of the novel
depends.

> Upon a cetain day in March Albinus got a long letter from him
> [Axel Rex, who is interested in helping Albinus], but *its arrival
> coincided with a sudden crisis in Albinus' private—very
> private—life*, so that the beautiful idea, which otherwise would
> have lingered on and perhaps found a wall on which to cling
> and blossom, had strangely faded and shriveled in the course of
> the last week. (LD, 11, italics mine)

The "sudden crisis" is, of course, Albinus' having met (or
more accurately, seen and been impressed by) Margot Peters,
who happened to be the usher on duty in a movie house to
which he had gone. That the letter from Rex expressing interest in Albinus' nascent project coincides with Albinus' first
visions of Margot deepens the "crisis"; Rex will perform the
function of animator, though not in the way Albinus initially
desired. Rex has, in fact, written in his letter that he would
accept "a fee of so much (a startling sum)... for designing say
a Breughel film—the 'Proverbs' for instance, or anything else
Albinus might like to have him set in motion" (LD, 11). The
metaphor of motion begins to become resonant at the end of
the chapter; Albinus thinks: "What the devil do I care for this fellow Rex, this idiotic conversation, this chocolate cream...?
I'm going mad and nobody knows it. And *I can't stop*, it's
hopeless trying, and tomorrow I'll go there [to the movie
house] again and sit like a fool in that darkness'" (LD, 13,
italics mine). Already Nabokov has begun to suggest the moral
implications of the use of the motion picture as the mode

through which the novel is to be perceived: it has to do with madness and the way in which an irresponsible desire can turn on the person who entertains it, finally controlling him as though he were indeed no more than an actor in a film whose role, as it were, plays him. And the chapter closes with Albinus' thinking in the most traditional melodramatic terms about the possible conclusion of the enmeshings of a love triangle: "No, you can't take a pistol and plug a girl you don't even know, simply because she attracts you" (LD, 13). The foreshadowing of the novel's conclusion is obvious.

The second chapter is equally suggestive. It is basically concerned with the contrast between the nature of Albinus' marriage and his desire for some other liaison. All the details given about his relationship with his wife, Elisabeth, are of a piece, suggesting, essentially, inertness. Albinus has a "slowish mind," he speaks with a "very slight hesitation"; his former affairs (before his marriage) have been "tedious," "of the heavyweight variety," involving women who were "cold" and "dreary." The summary adjective in the description is "feeble," and those girls of whom he has dreamed but has not known have "just slid past him." The woman he finally marries is pale and delicate, "a clinging little soul, docile and gentle," whose love, with rare exceptions, is "of the lily variety." If one combines with this focus on sluggishness, inertia, and docility the name "Albinus," one begins to take seriously the notion that before his meeting with Margot, his idea about animation, and his correspondence with Rex, Albinus has been living a colorless still life.

The other aspect of the polarity that Chapter 2 presents is Albinus' desire for something else, and this desire is focused on his brief visit to the movie house, where he first sees Margot. (The pivot on which the two aspects of Chapter 2 turn is the birth of Albinus' daughter, Irma.)[7] Again the description

7. I will discuss the implications of this at the close of part I.

Nabokov employs is important. There is motion within the cinema as well as on the screen, Margot is dressed in black (no lily), and she is, suggestively, his guide. It is in this chapter that the motion picture in which the characters in the novel act their roles can be said to begin. There is the location of Albinus' meeting with Margot in the movie house, the bringing together of the black and white (Albinus himself as well as the nature of his life up to this point, and the black usher leading him to his seat in the darkness) as though a negative has been created, and the introduction of motion into Albinus' life. But what is crucial are the two brief snippets from the movie Albinus watches after he sits down. He sees "a girl . . . receding among tumbled furniture before a masked man with a gun" and "a car . . . spinning down a smooth road with hairpin turns between cliff and abyss." For Albinus, and the reader at this point, "there was no interest whatever in watching happenings which he could not understand since he had not yet seen their beginning," but once the reader finishes the novel the importance of these two scenes, and the care with which they have been placed, become clear, though neither the importance nor the care dawns on Albinus.

These two brief scenes are from Albinus' experience later in the novel: the drive away from the hotel at Rouginard, on a winding road between cliff and abyss, which ends in the accident that causes Albinus' blindness, and the last full scene of the book in which he tries to murder Margot. Albinus is watching scenes from the motion picture that will become his life, and the ungentle, though subtle, irony of his not understanding these scenes "since he had not yet seen their beginning" is lost on him: he is at that precise moment involved in the first scenes of the film he watches.[8] That this is so is inten-

---

8. A fascinating detail may be adjunctive here. The poster outside the movie house portrays "a man looking up at a window framing a child in a nightshirt" (LD, 19–20). Such a man appears eventually (LD, 169–70); it is not Albinus, however,

sified by another sentence: "Had he not gone there that second time he might perhaps have been able to forget this ghost of an adventure, but now it was too late." The inevitability of his involvement is clear, but what is added is the nature of what he is involved in: *the ghost of an adventure*, which may be considered a concise definition of any particular instance of the celluloid art.[9]

Chapter 3, a flashback into Margot Peters' past, is made to perform several functions. First, the description of Margot is done in terms that serve to intensify the contrast, already implied, between her and Albinus' wife. She is "bright and high-spirited," an animated foil to the passive Elisabeth. Moreover, the crucial event in her past is her truncated affair with Axel Rex. Their fated[10] roles in Albinus' life, already suggested by the "coincidence" in Albinus' "very private life" in Chapter 1, has begun a good deal earlier than the present time of the novel. And Nabokov treats their initial affair in his usual skillful way. It seems that the "career" of Margot, in whose beginning Axel Rex is instrumental, will be nothing more than that of expensive whore. But there is more to it than that; the de-

---

but a stranger, probably the lover whom the "painted lady in a Spanish shawl" later admits (LD, 176). The fascination resides in 1) the fact that the girl in the nightshirt is Irma, and her peering from the open window at the man in the street brings on the severe chill that kills her—does the author, prior to his use of Conrad, intrude here to "cause" the fatal exposure?—and 2) the snow-covered, whistling man has echoes (almost certainly false) in both Rex and Albinus. The relevant passages appear on pages 145, 158, 162, and 175–76.

9. Other aspects of the novel seem conceived in line with the use of the film as the mode through which it is to be perceived. The profusion of chapters, their varied lengths, and especially the very brief ones, suggest a scenario. There are stage directions not only for the last scene but also on page 150. Twice the fictional technique suggests the use of a subliminal frame in a motion picture: the flash to the hockey game on page 170, when Rex meets Paul in the entrance to Albinus' apartment house, and in Margot's quick memory of Rex locking Frau Levandovsky in the lavoratory as she (Margot) locks Albinus in his bedroom, on page 62. The first three chapters make the past present by flashback, and the point of view from which the accident is handled (Chapter 32) suggests the cinematic technique of panning.

10. By the novelist. See part III of this chapter.

94

tails of their relationship are carefully fitted into the pattern of cinematic experience that informs the whole novel. Margot's liaison with Rex is inseparable, first, from art: she poses (I suppose one could say professionally) for art classes, and Rex's last gesture before he leaves is to sketch her lying on the bed. In addition, the whole chapter is laden with Margot's visions of herself as a movie star: "So the days passed and Margot had only a very vague idea of what she was really aiming at, though there was always that vision of herself as a screen beauty in gorgeous furs being helped out of a gorgeous car by a gorgeous hotel porter under a giant umbrella" (LD,30).[11] Finally, the apparent downward course of her ambition (from posing, to being rebuffed by film producers, to working as an usher in a cinema) is in reality a progression toward the one movie in which she will star, the love triangle of Margot, Rex, and Albinus. The chapter closes with her first direct meeting with Albinus, their first exchange of words, and the first reel of Nabokov's ghost of an adventure is under way.

There are two other particular items worth noting about the third chapter. First, Margot's vision of her gorgeous self escorted as screen star is fulfilled, though not in the terms she uses when she envisions it. The night she meets Albinus it is raining. "'You're drenched,' she said with a smile. He took the umbrella out of her hand; she pressed still closer to him" (LD, 43). Presumably Albinus has seen the same movie each time he has come to the cinema during this first, crucial week. It is the movie in which he is unwittingly one of the stars and in whose beginning he is currently involved. The repetition of the detail of the umbrella, significantly deflated from Margot's earlier version of it, is part of the pattern by which Nabokov signals the nature of the book. Second, the progression of

11. One of the aspects of parody is hyperbole; movies, too, present everything literally "larger than life." The terms of Margot's vision of herself conjoin nicely the form and purport of the novel.

Margot's "artistic" activities echoes Albinus' original idea of animating paintings. She is first sketched, as it were, anonymously, by art students, then by the man whom Albinus requests to assist in the animation project, Axel Rex. Then she meets Albinus in the opening scenes of the motion picture that is the novel.

I have gone into some detail with the first three chapters of *Laughter in the Dark* to try to show how thoroughly, from its beginning, Nabokov has committed the novel's form to the mode of the film. I will continue to follow this direction, but without maintaining as strict an allegiance to the chapter-by-chapter development of the book.

Throughout the rest of the novel Nabokov continues to employ phrases whose chief purpose seems to be to keep the reader alerted to the basic mode of perception through which he is being asked to view the experiences of its characters. Margot, for instance, often makes "all sorts of wonderful faces for the benefit of her dressing-chest mirror or recoil[s] before the barrel of an imaginary gun" (LD,69), the latter of which activities again figures in the end of the book. Before his wife discovers his infidelity and leaves him, Albinus covers frequent absences from home by saying his evenings out are "spent with some artists interested in the cinema idea of his" (LD, 70), a statement he considers a lie, but the unsettling truth of which the reader should be well aware. At the close of the scene in which Albinus leaves his otherwise deserted apartment, Frieda, the maid, sobs "in the wings" (LD,89); among the erotic gestures of Margot which please Albinus is the "gradual dimming of her eyes (as if they were being slowly extinguished like the lights in a theater)" (LD, 92); at the beach, Margot's bathing suit is "too short to be true" (LD,112); Margot views the sort of life Albinus could offer her as "full of the glamor of a first-class film with rocking palm trees and shuddering roses (for it is always windy in filmland)" (LD,118); at the Swiss villa

Rex eats "like a silent film diner" (LD, 162); and during one of the dinners which Axel and Margot share with Albinus this passage occurs:

> As she sat between these two men who were sharing her life, she felt as though she were the chief actress in a mysterious and passionate film-drama—so she tried to behave accordingly; smiling absently, drooping her eyelashes, tenderly laying her hand on Albinus' sleeve, as she asked him to pass the fruit, and casting a fleeting, indifferent glance at her former lover. (LD, 147)

But perhaps the best of these fillips to the reader's awareness occurs in Chapter 15, as Nabokov is describing the first days Margot spends in Albinus' flat.

> Late one night, as he was soaping Margot's back after a dance and she was amusing herself by standing in the full bath upon her enormous sponge (bubbles coming up as in a glass of champagne), she suddenly asked him whether he did not think she could become a film actress. (LD, 122)

The image of the actress in the glass of champagne, delight-fully undercut, is straight out of the golden age of the cinema, or, in a metaphoric mixture true to the nature of that age, the silver screen. And it appears here not only as a part of the pattern of cinematic experience that is the core of the book's meaning, but also in connection with Margot's broaching to Albinus the possibility that he finance a film in which she would act, which turns out to be a film within the film that is the novel.

It is with such an image that one begins to get the taste of parody, and to detect the implications of the use of the mode of motion pictures as the form by which the novel is structured. The "real-life" actress whom Nabokov refers to indicates the sort of movie he wants his reader to have in mind; that is, the mode of the film as a way of perceiving the meaning of the book is used both generally and specifically. The actress is Garbo, and the specific kind of film that comes to mind is the melodramatic tragedy of romantic intrigue.[12] The first suggestion of this occurs as Margot stands in the movie house watching Greta Garbo. The focus is sharpened in Chapter 8, in which Albinus makes his first entrance into the rooms Margot has rented and furnished at his expense. On his way to the flat, whose location he has learned by cutting through some of the lies Margot has told him about her past, he notices his surroundings.

> It was half past seven. Lights were being put on, and their soft orange glow looked very lovely in the pale dusk. The sky was still quite blue, with a single salmon-colored cloud in the distance, and all this unsteady balance between light and dusk made Albinus feel giddy.
> "In another moment I shall be in paradise," he thought, as he sped in a taxi over the whispering asphalt. (LD, 77)

The concatenation of suggestions in the passage is very effective. The hour is the hour when couples go to the cinema; the lights are soft, as in a theater before the film begins; Albinus uses a taxi, as per advertisements intended to appeal to light-hearted lovers on an evening out in a big city (this is Berlin). There is the traditional mindless sunset for sentimentalists mushing up the sky. Added to these suggestions, which are easy enough, is the effect his surroundings have on Albinus: the combination of light and dark makes him "giddy." That his perception, his taste, his aesthetic preferences, and his

12. When this discussion appeared in *Tri-Quarterly*, the following note occurred at this point: "Because of the fun made with the name—Dorianna Karenina—of the leading lady in the film that Albinus finances, one might guess even more specifically that a particular movie is to be invoked, Garbo's *Anna Karenina.*" Nabokov commented on my note later: "The film in which my heroine is given a small part in the 1920's has nothing to do with Garbo's *Anna Karenina* (of which incidently I have only seen stills), but what I would like my readers to brood over is my singular power of prophecy, for the name of the leading lady (Dorianna Karenina) in the picture invented by me in 1928 prefigured that of the actress (Anna Karina) who was to play Margot forty years later in the film *Laughter in the Dark*" (SO, 287).

moral sense are indeed unsteady, is, in effect, proved by his being able to accept the apartment when he enters it. "Margot was lying in a kimono on a dreadful chintz-covered sofa, her arms crossed behind her head. On her stomach an open book was poised, cover upward" (LD, 77–78). The confusion over the letter Margot has sent Albinus, which is being delivered even as the two lovers talk about it, the perplexity this causes Albinus, Margot's cool indifference to his dilemma, and Albinus' futile dash across Berlin to intercept the letter are all of a piece with the best (or worst) of the frantic stylized melodrama of the cinema of the twenties and thirties. In addition to the caricatured scene there are two details which deepen one's sense of the mode Nabokov is using to condition the reader's perception of the chapter. First, as Albinus ends his trip to try to intercept the ominous letter: "He arrived, he jumped out, he paid as men do in films—blindly thrusting out a coin" (LD, 80). Second, as Margot reacts to Albinus' potential hysteria: "She shrugged her shoulders, picked up the book and turned her back on him. On the right-hand page was a photographic study of Greta Garbo" (LD, 79). And the chapter ends this way:

> She let the book slip to the floor and smiled as she looked at his downcast twitching face. *It was time to act, she supposed.*
>
> Margot stretched herself out, was aware of a pleasant tingling in her slim body, and said, gazing up at the ceiling, "Come here."
>
> He came, sat down on the edge of the couch and shook his head despondently.
>
> "Kiss me," she said, closing her eyes. "I'll comfort you."
> (LD, 82, italics mine)

Fadeout. The whole chapter seems to me superbly done, uniting for the first time in the novel the mode of the cinema as the perspective from which the novel is to be viewed, the essential parodic intention of the use of the mode, and the moral suggestions implicit in the parody. Albinus, caught in the exaggerated melodrama of the film experience he is in part the creator of, is quite blind long before the automobile accident puts him in the condition which physically acknowledges the moral fact.

As with the series of details I listed earlier in connection with Nabokov's continual reminders to the reader of the perceptual mode of the novel, so in connection with the parodic importance of the same mode: in a scene of reconciliation between Margot and Albinus we read, "'And you really don't despise me?' she asked, smiling through her tears, which was difficult, seeing there were no tears to smile through" (LD, 100); when Albinus, still with his secret more or less intact, converses with Margot's brother, the narrator says, "Indeed, there was a fine flavor of parody about this talk" (LD, 105); and, later, when Rex gets a button on his jacket caught in the lace of Margot's dress while he is trying to kiss her before Albinus returns to the room:

> Rex was about to raise himself, but at the same moment he noticed that a button of his coat was caught in the lace on Margot's shoulder. Margot tried to disentangle it swiftly. Rex tugged, but the lace refused to give way. Margot grunted in dismay, as she pulled at the knot with her sharp shiny nails. At that moment Albinus swept into the room.
> "No, I'm not embracing Fraulein Peters," said Rex coolly. "I was only making her comfortable and got entangled, you see."
> Margot was still worrying the lace without raising her lashes. The situation was farcical in the extreme and Rex was enjoying it hugely.
> Albinus silently drew out a fat penknife with a dozen blades and opened what turned out to be a small file. He tried again and broke his nail. The burlesque was developing nicely. (LD, 164–65)

The terms *farcical* and *burlesque*, along with Rex's awareness of the nature of the scene in which he is snagged, leads one to the passages dealing directly with the subject of caricature, passages in which the novel theorizes about itself. Rex is, basically, a caricaturist himself, and, "to say the least of it, a cynic" (LD, 142).

> As a child he had poured oil over live mice, set fire to them and watched them dart about for a few seconds like flaming meteors. And it is best not to inquire into the things he did to cats. Then, in riper years, when his artistic talent developed, he tried in more subtle ways to satiate his curiosity, for it was not anything morbid with a medical name—oh, not at all,—just cold, wide-eyed curiosity, just the marginal notes supplied by life to his art. It amused him immensely to see life made to look silly, as it slid hopelessly into caricature. He despised practical jokes: he liked them to happen by themselves with perchance now and then just that little touch on his part which would send the wheel running downhill. (LD, 142–43)

The paradigmatic "practical joke" Nabokov gives as representative of the sort of humor that appeals to Rex is revealing as it reverberates among the actual happenings of the experience Rex is involved in in the novel: "Thus goes the Hegelian syllogism of humor. Thesis: Uncle made himself up as a burglar (a laugh for the children); antithesis: it *was* a burglar (a laugh for the reader); synthesis: it still was Uncle (fooling the reader)" (LD, 143). This brief dialectic loosely parallels the structure of the "joke" that happens to Albinus, in which Rex adds his "little touch": Albinus dresses himself up as lover in a film; it *is* a lover in the film; it is, as the bullet enters the flesh, still Albinus. In the transmutation of the paradigm into Albinus' experience the moral implications of the "joke" become somewhat more apparent. The thesis involves an irresponsible sense of becoming involved in a game which has no consequences: one can fool oneself at the outset by thinking one has control over the outcome, as Albinus attempts to do when he considers "plugging" the chick before he has even spoken to her. In fact, after he is committed to the affair, Albinus is still able to consider the easy way out: "She is still my wife and I love her, and I shall, of course, shoot myself if she dies by my fault" (LD,91). The antithesis involves the reader's seeing how completely the film role engulfs Albinus, and he is fooled by the synthesis in the sense that, having congratulated himself on seeing the cinematic nature of Albinus' experience, he forgets the "real" Albinus, who does, indeed, for all practical purposes, shoot himself.[13] The structure of the book is such, in other words, that the reader may tend to forget the actor in the role, and pay attention to only the role itself, as Albinus himself does. The Rexian joke, then, is on both Albinus and the reader.

I am not sure how far one can push such an analogy; I do think, however, the general relationship is there, and it is stressed almost immediately in the text by this sentence: "The art of caricature, as Rex understood it, was thus based (apart from its synthetic, fooled-again nature) on the contrast between cruelty on one side and credulity on the other" (LD, 144). The simple connection here is Rex-cruelty, Albinus-credulity; the more complicated implications of the pairings I will discuss in part II.

The dependence of the novel's parodic intention on the mode of the motion picture as the perspective from which it is to be viewed, and the implications suggested by the parody, which are given a theoretical base in the comments on Rex's ideas about caricature, are focused in three notable instances.

First in Albinus' recollection of the accident: "A sharp jerk of the steering wheel to avoid [the cyclists]—and up the car dashed, mounting a pile of stones on the right, and in the next

---

13. See Carol T. Williams' comments on this pattern in "Nabokov's Dialectical Structure," *Wisconsin Studies in Contemporary Literature* (Spring, 1967), 250–67. Rex's "burglar" joke is itself echoed in the body of the novel when Albinus tries to explain Margot's presence in his apartment to Paul by saying a burglar had locked him in the bathroom. In keeping with the paradigm of dialectic, Margot *does* become a burglar in effect, as she and Rex rapidly reduce Albinus' bank account after the accident.

fraction of that second, a telegraph post loomed in front of the windscreen. Margot's outstretched arm had flown across the picture—and the next moment the magic lantern went out" (LD, 240). The terminology by which Albinus' perception is presented is part of the film mode of the novel, and the association of the magic lantern with Albinus' consciousness makes clear one metaphorical direction in which the film mode is to be taken. One would expect the movie to end when the lantern goes out, but the dark chamber suggested by the Russian title of the novel, *Kamera Obskura*, works against this allegorical limitation. It is also quite fitting, in terms of the sense of moral fate the novel is partly concerned with, that Nabokov suggests here that the movie has taken over Albinus' experience; if it has not been clear before, it is obvious after the accident that any idea Albinus had about controlling his own destiny is pure illusion. And there is a corollary to this. One might expect that since his credulous vision had gotten Albinus into his predicament, perhaps the removal of that vision would bring with it some kind of insight: the trite idea of a blind man knowing himself, and "reality," better than the man whose ability to see helps him keep appearances between himself and the truth. But it doesn't happen this way: Albinus "could not always succeed in convincing himself that physical blindness was spiritual vision; in vain did he try to cheat himself with the fancy that his life with Margot was now happier, deeper and purer, and in vain did he concentrate on the thought of her touching devotion" (LD, 257–58).

The consideration leads into the second point; the following passage occurs in the context of the statement about physical and spiritual blindness:

> Albinus now became conscious that he had not really been different from a certain narrow specialist at whom he used to scoff: from the workman who knows only his tools, or the virtuoso who is only a fleshly accessory of his violin. Albinus' specialty

had been his passion for art; his most brilliant discovery had
been Margot. But now, all that was left of her was a voice, a
rustle and a perfume; it was as though she had returned to the
darkness of the little cinema from which he had once with-
drawn her. (LD, 257)

In terms of the book's structure, this is exactly what has happened. One of the scenes—the car on the winding road—that
Albinus saw in the movie which was playing at the cinema
where he first saw Margot has already been realized in his own
life; the book is turning back on itself. And the darkness inside
which he moves becomes again the darkness of the cinema. It
is in great part his own perception, his imaginative way of making his shabby and irresponsible affair with Margot take on the
sheen of a Garbo movie, which has got him where he is.
Again, his loss of eyesight is a physical acknowledgment of a
moral fact.

The third such instance in which the implications of the
parody are focused is the viewing of Margot's film, which occupies the whole of Chapter 23. Everyone at the viewing except Albinus is able to see what a horrid actress Margot is. Seeing the film could have been a key to Margot's "real" nature
for Albinus, but a blind man can't see. And while the screen-
ing of Margot's film is in progress Rex, who is bored, "closed
his eyes, saw the little colored caricatures he had been doing
lately for Albinus, and meditated over the fascinating though
quite simple problem of how to suck some more cash out of
him" (LD, 190). Margot acts in the film as she acts in the affair
with Albinus, and Rex's thought about the caricatures serves to
focus the association between the two contexts, as well as to
suggest Albinus' thorough credulity.

To return, finally, to Irma's birth, which I mentioned previously as the pivot on which the polarity of Chapter 2 turns, I
would like to make one or two suggestions about the way in
which the perceptual mode of the novel, the film, is made to

include characters other than the members of the triangle. First of all, Albinus' thoughts while he waits in the hospital for the baby to be born are presented in terms that set his perception of the event in the cinematic basis of the rest of his experience. Just as the doctor announces the birth, "before Albinus' eyes there appeared a fine dark rain, like the flickering of some very old film (1910, a brisk jerky funeral procession with legs moving too fast)" (LD, 18). The doctor's announcement has been, to say the least, enigmatical: "At length the assistant surgeon emerged and said gloomily: 'Well, it's all over'" (LD, 18). That might, indeed, make a prospective father, haggard and worried, think of a funeral, but only an art historian and restorer of paintings who has a tendency to view his life as though it were a motion picture would respond in the terms Albinus does.

This is interesting in itself, since it reveals Albinus' penchant for the distancing of reality through art before he begins his liaison with Margot, but Albinus echoes the doctor's words later in the novel, making Irma's birth resonant with his death. He says, after the bullet penetrates his side, "So that's all" (LD, 291). It is as though the process of viewing life—all of it, not just the affair with Margot—as a motion picture began with the birth of Irma; and, further, that Albinus' death occurred at Irma's birth.[14] I mean that figuratively, of course:

---

14. Chapters 20 and 21, which deal with Irma's death, expand this focus somewhat, suggesting as they do that Margot is, for Albinus, among her other aspects, also a child, a substitute for Irma. The dialogue which opens Chapter 22 sharpens this possibility: Albinus says to Margot, "You're a child yourself" (LD, 180). Margot has turned the nursery in Albinus' flat into a ping-pong room, which suggests something about the way Albinus' life has been transformed into a game whose rules have nothing to do with paternal responsibility. As he stands in the ping-pong room, almost at the point of giving up his affair and returning to his wife, he "listlessly took up a small celluloid ball and let it bounce, but instead of thinking of his child he saw another figure, a graceful, lively, wanton girl, laughing, one heel raised, as she thrust out her ping-pong bat" (LD, 178). Further, as Albinus tries to console Margot during her tantrums over her bad performance in the film, he "used the very words with which he had once comforted Irma when he kissed a bruise—words which now, after Irma's death, were

once Albinus began to conceive his life as a film he then began to live a parody of himself, which could be said to be a kind of death the rest of the novel fulfills. Elisabeth herself, when she is first described, may be seen, then, through Albinus' eyes as part of a motion picture. The black and white contrast between her and Margot adds to this possibility, as does the inclusion of Otto in a conversation that has about it "a fine flavor of parody." Thus, the whole world of the novel, as seen by Albinus, and not simply his relationship with Rex and Margot, is conceived in the mode of the film.

II   ALBINUS REX

Nabokov has said that "Satire is a lesson, parody is a game."[15] *Laughter in the Dark* is no less a game than any other fiction he has written; I hope the sense of that game, of details placed as pieces in a puzzle, of echoes and interpenetrations, has been apparent in my comments thus far. At the same time, as I have been trying to show, the game is so played as to imply certain moral, aesthetic, and perceptual concerns; Nabokov's novels and stories are by no means moralizing—far from it, and that is part of one's delight in reading them—but they are involved with moral predicaments on which their very structure comments.

He has also said, "There are no 'real' doubles in my novels," and, speaking of *Laughter* specifically, "A lover can be viewed as the betrayed party's double but that is pointless."[16] What I am going to do now, in the teeth of those remarks, is discuss the relationship implied between Albinus and Axel Rex in *Laughter*; the problem set by Nabokov's comments becomes to

---

vacant" (LD, 192). The Englishwoman's comment when she sees Albinus and Margot frolicking on the beach—"Look at that German romping about with his daughter"— also seems part of this pattern.

15. Appel interview (SO, 75).
16. SO, 83.

talk about that relationship without slipping into the traditional—à la Dostoevsky, for instance, or Stevenson—assumption of the existence of "real" doubles. [17]

One might begin with a passage to which I have already referred: "Thus the art of caricature, as Rex understood it, was based . . . on the contrast between cruelty on the one side and credulity on the other." This in itself suggests only a kind of pairing, not doubling; Rex is cruel, Albinus credulous. And when one takes the passage in the context of Albinus' idea of the animation of still life, and that idea's fulfillment in the novel, one can see that both Rex and Albinus are necessary to its realization: Albinus has the idea, Rex supplies the motion. This mutual dependence is further suggested by the names of the two characters: Albinus, a pale and passive man, and Rex, a masterful, active one; Albinus in some sense a freak snared in the trap of inertia, and Axel Rex, both king and that around which motion is centered. [18] Further, there is a foiling of the professional functions of the two men: Albinus is a restorer of old paintings, Rex a forger of them.

None of these details points toward doubling of characters in any sense, but when they are seen in concert with other suggestions made in the course of the novel one has to follow the path a little farther. Albinus' last name, for instance, is used by only one character *in* the novel (Schiffermiller, pp. 285 and 287), yet the narrator prefers to use that appellation almost exclusively. Why the discrepancy, one wonders in passing. Perhaps to suggest, among the other possibilities I've mentioned, by repeated use of the name with a Latin ending a

17. The value of *that* assumption I will confront in the next chapter.

18. There are two spots where the Axel-axle association—axle as a moving center causing radiant motion—is suggested beyond the audial hint: "Margot suddenly gave a sob and turned away. [Rex] pulled her by the sleeve, but she turned away still farther. They revolved in one spot" (LD,135); "He despised practical jokes; he liked them to happen by themselves with perchance now and then just that little touch on his part which would send the wheel running downhill" (LD,143).

connection with the Latin word that serves as the name of Albinus' rival? Add to this the manner in which the narrator describes the general response Margot has to the two men: "And
she liked Miller enormously" (LD, 35), "and she quite liked
Albinus" (LD, 68); the point at which "Albinus marveled at
his own divided nature" (LD, 46); and this rather pointed passage in Chapter 27: "She [Margot] needed only one man—
Rex. And Rex was Albinus' shadow" (LD, 207–208). Confronted with such an accumulation, one is sorely tempted to
say that something beyond simple foiling is at stake.

Yet if this were all, one could still possibly drop the matter.
But it isn't. There are two other aspects of the way the two men
are treated that make the problem (if it's a problem) even more
difficult to evade. First, one recalls the mysterious whistler in
the snowy street (a character reminiscent of "Mr. M'Intosh"),
whose resonant quality I have already mentioned (in note 8).
Second, and most tantalizing of all, is the fact that Rex and
Albinus adopt, independently of each other (but not of their
creator), similar pseudonyms when they try to disguise their
identity from Margot: Rex chooses "Miller," which Albinus
embroiders to "Schiffermiller." [19] It is, in fact, the introduction of a person named Schiffermiller, a character apparently
separate from both Rex and Albinus, that thoroughly complicates the whole idea of possible doubles. This "final" Schiffermiller is house porter at the building containing Albinus'
flat; he speaks to Albinus on the phone, repeating a function
Udo Conrad performed for Albinus earlier (see section III),
and he admits Albinus to the building where the final tête à

19. There is a good possibility that lepidoptera are involved in the pattern of the
novel's meaning: a miller is a kind of moth. I don't have the equipment to develop
this. Nor can I do anything more than point out the chance that the Black-White
drama between the two kings of a chess game is operating in the play between Rex,
Albinus, and the reader.

tête with Margot occurs. Is Schiffermiller another authorial
agent, lubricating the plot? Is he an external echo of Albinus'
internal ability to figure out the last place Margot might be? Is
he simply a retroactive intrusion that "explains" where Albinus
got his pseudonym to begin with? He is what is known as a
"minor" character, yet he is called by the name the "main"
character in the novel has used to disguise himself. It is all very
convoluted and tricky, and it is indeed possible that Nabokov
intends the reader of the novel to make a fool of himself, [20]
after the manner of Rex's idea of the effect of caricature, as I am
doing now, by seeking the resolution of a pattern where no
resolution is possible. A skillful detective story writer knows red
herrings are as important as real clues. [21]

There is no doubt that Axel Rex is a character who exists
separately from Albert Albinus (as, for instance, Smurov is *not*
physically separate from the "I" of *The Eye*); but there also
seems no doubt that one is intended to entertain the possibility
that Rex and Albinus interpenetrate in some way. There is at
least the chance that one is intended to see Rex as embodying
qualities which Albinus would himself like to possess, particularly Rex's mobility and his success with women. And perhaps
this toying with the possibility of their being doubles is a means
to intensify the mutual dependence that is absolutely necessary
for the fulfillment of their functions as characters in the inexorable *formal* destiny of the novel.

20. That dimension is itself a bit complicated. While discussing the double business in the earlier version of this chapter I had noted that "Margot discovers Albinus'
address by . . . finding [his last name] in the telephone book under 'R'." (For Rex, of
course.) Nabokov's response to that point (SO, 288) is puzzling, implying as it does
that in the 1936 *Laughter in the Dark* the Albinus character had a name beginning
with R. As far as I can tell, the character was first called "Kretschmar," in connection
with which Nabokov acknowledged a small, coy revenge in *Speak, Memory* (134).
This is a genuine circle, from which I don't see an extrication.

21. In much-noted passages, Nabokov speaks of nature and art as games "of intricate enchantment and deception"; see *Speak, Memory*, pages 125 and 290–91.

This latter possibility brings one to the edge of another dimension of *Laughter in the Dark* which further complicates it, and turns its parodic implications back upon itself.

III   UDO CONRAD

I have been talking about the idea of animating paintings by old masters as though it originated with Albinus. It did not. "It so happened that one night Albinus had a beautiful idea. True, it was not quite his own, as it had been suggested by a phrase in Conrad (not the famous Pole, but Udo Conrad who wrote the *Memoirs of a Forgetful Man* and that other thing about the old conjuror who spirited himself away at his farewell performance)" (LD,7). The latter of those two books by Udo Conrad is mentioned again, by title, when authorial techniques are discussed at a party in Albinus' flat. The whole passage is revealing.

> "I don't know, gentlemen, what you think of Udo Conrad," said Albinus, joining in the fray. "It would seem to me that he is that type of author with exquisite vision and a divine style which might please you, Herr Rex, and that if he isn't a great writer it is because—and here, Herr Baum, I am with you—he has a contempt for social problems which, in this age of social upheavals, is disgraceful and, let me add, sinful. I knew him well in my student days, as we used to meet now and then. I consider his best book to be *The Vanishing Trick*, the first chapter of which, as a matter of fact, he read here, at this table—I mean—well—at a similar table and . . . " (LD,132–33)

Udo Conrad is, to use a figure appropriate to the controlling focus of *Laughter in the Dark*, an ectype of Vladimir Nabokov. The original of Conrad's *Memoirs* is Nabokov's *Speak, Memory;*[22] *Invitation to a Beheading*, of all his books

22. There may be a problem here. *Kamera Obskura* was written in 1931, and the first English version, translated by Winifred Roy—"insufficiently revised by me," Nabokov has said (Appel interview, SO, p. 82) —appeared in 1936, the year in which Nabokov established the order of chapters for *Speak, Memory* and wrote and published the first of these, "Mademoiselle O," Chapter 5 of the finished work (see the foreword

the one Nabokov held in "greatest esteem,"[23] lurks behind Conrad's *The Vanishing Trick*. The "similar table" probably still exists somewhere in an anonymous room in Berlin, with an almost palpable ghost still seated at it. Further, Albinus' critical remarks reproduce in small, as do the criticisms of Sebastian Knight's books in that novel, the two most frequent judgments made about Nabokov's fiction;[24] the phrases "exquisite vision" and "divine style" are more than dinner table effusions, suggesting as they do Nabokov's constant concern with the nature of perception and the author's relationship to the books he writes.

The concern with this relationship, and the attempt to make it a conscious part of the experience of a given novel, was not new for Nabokov when he wrote the Russian original of *Laughter* in 1931. He, as Blavdak Vinomori (accompanied by his wife), had made "visits of inspection" in the last two chapters of *King, Queen, Knave* (1928),[25] and in that same novel he had not only appeared in another anagrammatical disguise—as Mr. Vivian Badlook, the photographer—but also in the ectypes of Goldemar (the author of a play and screenplay called *King, Queen, Knave*), old Enricht (Franz's landlord), young Vivian on his tricycle, and both the professor who created the mannikins and Mr. Ritter, who contracted to buy them.[26] And he has continued to use the technique, the

---

to *Speak, Memory*). Nabokov himself "Englished" *Laughter in the Dark* for Bobbs-Merrill in 1938, and the edition I'm using was brought out by New Directions in 1960. Given Nabokov's gamesmanship, it is quite likely that, as early as the 1936 English version of the novel, he is referring to one of his own books, although at that time only one chapter of it had been completed.

23. SO, 92.

24. See (on pages 287–88 of SM) Nabokov's remarks about the critical response among Russian émigrés in Berlin to the work of V. Sirin, which is to say himself.

25. See the foreword to that novel (New York: McGraw-Hill, 1968), vii.

26. Two of the characters from *King, Queen, Knave* play the shortest of phantomic parts in *Laughter in the Dark*: when Albinus returns to his flat after his family has departed, he finds in the mail "an invitation for lunch from the Dreyers" (LD, 86).

most obvious examples being Vivian Darkbloom in *Lolita* and Vivian Bloodmark in *Speak, Memory*.

These figures are *not* Nabokov—none of them is complex enough, for one thing—but signals of the presence of the authorial control without which no fiction is, or can be, written. In the case of *Laughter* Conrad's presence immediately makes one aware that no idea originates with the characters in a novel; thus one knows, or should know, from the beginning of the book that an important part of reading the novel is the reader's consciousness of what I would call the authorial presence, the controlling intelligence that is at work in every facet of the book. Things happen because the author makes them happen; the challenge for the author, in which he asks the reader to participate, is to make them happen according to an inexorable logic implanted in the structure of the book. Everything is not permitted—the author is not an aesthetic anarchist—and he asks the reader to test the formal demands of the composition the author has played in the initial writing of the book.

With this in mind, then, one sees that Conrad's personal appearances (in Chapters 27, 28, and 29) perform a parodic function, directing the overall parody of the novel toward the novel itself, and the authorial control over the novel. For Nabokov has a technical problem to solve in the chapters in which Conrad appears: it is time for Albinus to discover that he is being betrayed by Margot and Rex, and the author needs some way of communicating to him the truth of the situation about which he is deluded. Who knows the truth besides Margot and Rex, neither of whom could be expected to spoil a good thing by tattling? The author. So *he* appears, or more accurately through Udo Conrad acknowledges his presence, and himself imparts to Albinus the crucial information.[27] The

27. Kurt Dreyer at a similarly crucial juncture in *King, Queen, Knave* (Chapter 9) receives like prodding toward truth from a former mistress. (He keeps pushing intru-

formal machinery of the novel, in short, is uncovered at this point: what saves it from creaking is Nabokov's integration of the problem into the meaning of the novel, or the experience of reading the novel. He extends the parody that is being directed toward the characters in the novel to include the author (and the reader) of the novel. To use the terms with which I began this chapter, he acknowledges, as part of this particular book's fiber, the essentially parodic nature of fiction itself.

Conrad's appearance and the function he performs remind the reader of his involvement in artifice, in an imaginative experience that can be, by its nature, nothing except parody. It is no wonder that there are people whom parody upsets; I would guess that the more conscious the person the greater the possible upset, and the more possibly creative and rewarding it might be. If, as this novel and the two I have previously discussed in some detail imply, human perception is inevitably imaginative, then one is faced with the deduction that all perceptual constructions, whether they are embodied in a novel or not, are parodies, and that the assumption that a human being lives in and can apprehend a comfortable "factual" reality is the most disturbing parody of all.

---

sive Vivian and his trike away, but they will not be denied.) As my references indicate, *King, Queen, Knave* and *Laughter in the Dark* are, like *Bend Sinister* and *Invitation to a Beheading*, kissing cousins, as it were. In *King, Queen, Knave*, however, the machinery creaks more often and more noticeably. This is intentional; the formal analogue that functions in that novel is the puppet show, and Mr. Ritter's mannikins are, of course, center stage. They fail, finally, to operate themselves on their own steam, and dramatize thereby the fate their novel (and any novel) suffers: it runs down. *King, Queen, Knave* the novel even needs the buttressing of precedent and variant: there is the play *King, Queen, Knave* (attended some years back by the Dreyers) and *King, Queen, Knave* the movie (in progress, as is the theater in which it will be shown—a house of cards).

FIVE

Tinker to Evers
to Chance:
The Novel as Joke

I DOUBLE PLAY

The dead end to which my brief comments on Albinus Rex led me isn't the only such alleyway in Nabokov's works. It is similarly tantalizing, and "pointless," for example, to follow Humbert Humbert and Clare Quilty in the direction of their possible doubling, because of and in spite of their little tangle in Pavor Manor where the pronouns go mad. The psychological expunging that I will suggest as a possibility in *Pnin* exists without recourse to *doppelgänger*, and there is only one parasite in *Pale Fire*, though he fastens himself nominally to multiple objects, including a royal dream. There *are*, in short, no "real" doubles in Nabokov's fiction—no William Wilsons, Jekyll/Hydes or Yakov Petrovich Golyadkins; in fact, early in his career Nabokov composed an entire novel built on the parody and eventual rejection of such a tactic. In *Despair*— written in 1932, published in Russian in 1936—Hermann Hermann seeks in the classic manner to free himself from himself by killing a double he fancies he has fortuitously discovered; unlike the three gentlemen mentioned above, he

115

fails, having been deluded to begin with, and it is in the failure that the judgment not only of the literary device of doubles but the conception of doubles as a perceptual act, resides.[1]

From the early parts of the novel it is clear that Hermann's powers of observation are at least somewhat limited. He sees and reports what is too obvious to ignore: lipstick in Ardalion's pocket, Lydia in Ardalion's bed. Whether willfully or willy-nilly, however, he fails to draw the logical conclusion about the relationship between his wife and her cousin. Given this psychological obtuseness, it is not surprising that more obscure "evidence" eludes him altogether, though its presence in his narrative is probably intended to indicate how thoroughly preoccupied he is with the affair he won't, or doesn't, consciously face up to.[2]

The two riddles, for instance, are revealing.[3] The answers to each focus on aspects of Hermann's ruin, commercial and domestic. The contexts of each riddle, moreover, echo each other: Lydia is in bed both times, in the first instance inactively with her husband (she goes to sleep while he talks), and in the second relaxing after a tumble with Ardalion that Hermann has interruptus . . . ah . . . mmm; Ardalion is a part of the conversation the first time, is present the second; both cases involve, just prior to the riddle, a discussion of Hermann's being overworked and tired. And, as if the implications aren't blatant

---

1. *Despair* is a compendium of parody. A few of its objects are Freud, Dostoevsky, Turgenev, *A Portrait of the Artist as a Young Man*, the "well-made" novel, the epistolary novel, diaries, and memoirs. The extent of the play in connection with Dostoevsky, for instance, is suggested by the large number of pages on which reference or allusion occurs: 98, 187, 190, 198, 199, 211. Further, "dusty" and "dusky," epithets for Dostoevsky on some occasions, appear resonantly as adjectives on 118, 218, and 221. *Despair* is the novel where Nabokov's constant flirtation with the tour de force most closely approaches a full-blown affair.

2. It is also central to the game the author (distinct from the narrator) is playing with the reader.

3. Pages 60 and 115. All page references are to *Despair* (New York: G. P. Putnam's Sons, 1966).

enough, Lydia's riddle flaunts her affair[4] and, to judge from his reference to "Ardalion" in the narration, Hermann picks up and coyly communicates its answer.

Just as lost on Hermann are the implications of his attention to a still life he has seen in Tarnitz (D,79), which he thinks briefly Ardalion has painted. He asks Ardalion about it—"a tobacco pipe, on green cloth, and two roses"—during the second riddle scene (D,114), after he has discovered Lydia "on Ardalion's bed, half dressed—that is, shoeless and wearing only a rumpled green slip... smoking," and after he has watched Ardalion poke at his pipe. The still life in question, as a visit to Ardalion's landlady's room proves, is "not quite two roses and not quite a pipe, but a couple of large peaches and a glass ashtray." The sexual connection with the flowers and the fruit need not be labored, I think; what is remarkable is the way the business with the paintings dramatizes the length to which Hermann will go to divert his attention.

That desperation also leads him to think he is slandering his wife to Orlovius (D,143) and deceiving the lawyer as well, when in fact he is telling the truth and confirming "certain things" Orlovius has "long observed." He throws a similar boomerang when he offers the following illustration that Lydia is "little observant": "We discovered one day that to her the term 'mystic' was somehow dimly connected with 'mist' and 'mistake' and 'stick,' but that she had not the least idea what a mystic really was" (D,33). His own mistake with the missed stick is, of course, more crucial than Lydia's difficulty with the meaning of a word.

4. The first riddle is stimulated by Hermann's hearing a sound: "Chock," he says. The riddle follows: "My first is that sound, my second is an exclamation, my third will be prefixed to me when I'm no more; and my whole is my ruin." The answer is 1) chock 2) oh 3) late, or "chocolate," which Hermann manufactures. Lydia proposes the second riddle: "My first is a romantic fiery feeling. My second is a beast. My whole is a beast, too, if you like—or else a dauber." Answer: 1) Ardor 2) Lion, or Ardalion, her lover, and a painter. (Among the other meanings of *daub* are "soil, smear, defile.")

I have gone into this brief detail about selected instances of Hermann's obtuseness in order to give some indication of the situation in which he concocts his scheme involving Felix Wohlfahrt, why he would—continuing to speak of him as if he were a human being with motivation, that being part of the basic illusion—so completely and easily delude himself into thinking Felix looks enough like him for the plan to succeed. He is, as it were, dusty with desperation.

The simple fact, however, on which the parody and evaluation of the use of a double depends, is that no one else in the novel notices a resemblance between Hermann and Felix. Explicitly, Felix doesn't see it (D,21–22), the reporters and policemen don't see it (D, 196), Ardalion doesn't see it (D, 215). Implicitly, neither does Lydia (D, 215). There never is a double in *Despair*, then, only Hermann's desire for one.[5] I have sketched the context of that desire and its possible causes; as that context indicates, it is an intense desire. The passages that reveal that intensity, however, also lead toward the basis for the repudiation of the idea of the double, which are not merely aesthetic, but epistemological and moral as well.

Before I go into that, however, I want to confront the possibility that what is sufficient for me may not be sufficient for others. I find the denial by other observers in the novel of Felix's and Hermann's resemblance enough to characterize the "double" motif of *Despair* as Hermann's delusion. Coupled with other reasons (which I have mentioned) that one shouldn't trust the novel's narrator, the presence of this delusion leads me in the direction I have specified, toward parody. *Within* the novel the idea of the double is patently bogus, and issues in rather unsettling consequences; in the experience of reading, which adds the further dimension of the reader to the locus named "novel," it follows that to take the notion of the

5. Which desire the reader shares. "Felix in *Despair* is really a *false* double," Nabokov said in his 1966 interview with Alfred Appel (SO,84).

double seriously—or to be taken in by it—is to share Hermann's delusion.

The temptation, at this point, is to explain or diagnose Hermann's situation by means of one or another prearranged patterns that are taken from intellectual disciplines which on occasion are used to supplant the fiction on which they are wielded as critical tools. For instance, quite early in the book Nabokov prepares a wide and well-greased chute down which the psychologically oriented reader may slide. Hermann recounts the "dissociation" which began to occur a few months before his trip to Prague.

> I would be in bed with Lydia...winding up the brief series of preparatory caresses she was supposed to be entitled to, when all at once I would become aware that imp Split had taken over. My face was buried in the folds of her neck, her legs had started to clamp me, the ashtray toppled off the bed table, the universe followed—but at the same time, incomprehensibly and delightfully, I was standing naked in the middle of the room, one hand resting on the back of the chair where she had left her stockings and panties. The sensation of being in two places at once gave me an extraordinary kick. (D, 37)

The "kick" increases as Hermann increases the distance between himself as watcher and himself as lover. The metaphor of the theater takes over his prose and he imagines the optimal seat from which to observe the show located in "some remote upper gallery in a blue mist under the swimming allegories of the starry vault." The best he can manage, however, is the console in the parlor, a distance of "fifteen rows of seats," and the whole experience comes to a jolting halt one night when he is

> looking forward to an especially good show—which, indeed, had already started, with my acting self in colossal form and most inventive—from the distant bed, where I thought I was, came Lydia's yawn and voice stupidly saying that if I were not yet coming to bed, I might bring her the red book she had left in the parlor. It lay, in fact, on the console near my chair, and

119

rather than bring it I threw it bedward with a windmill flapping of pages. (D,38)

He tries to recapture the split but fails, though he says, "Perhaps [I] would have at last succeeded, had not a new and wonderful obsession obliterated in me all desire to resume those amusing but rather banal experiments" (D,39). The new and wonderful obsession, of course, is Felix. "Ah hah," the reader might exclaim at this point, "the externalization of part of the patient's self: schizophrenia." The convenience of succumbing to such a temptation is that the rest of the novel becomes unnecessary, or instead of a fiction with its own peculiar logic it becomes a clinical study of a particular mental aberration, a record instead of an invention. I think my rejection of this is more than a temperamental preference for the miracle of the prepared surprise over the predictable conclusion derived from a complex of symptoms. What the novel takes seriously is first the fantasy itself, and second the reflection of that fantasy in various literary mirrors. The reader might like to find the fantasy and the reflections imitating each other exactly, and as a corollary be able to use a psychological interpretation of the fantasy to render the novel's importance and meaning in a structure it could be said the novelist himself might give credence to. But in *Despair* the fantasy has no reflection—Hermann on the hill outside Prague is *not* Golyadkin on the Ismailovsky Bridge, or William Wilson confronting his conscience after an orgy of gambling—and because of this becomes parodic. A psychological interpretation of a situation that is itself a parody can be done, of course, but it seems at best foolish.[6] What it is at worst I think Nabokov suggests in the marvelous repudiation of the mechanical

6. My focus on the psychological interpretation here is representative; I have singled out my example because it is the easiest one to specify clearly. Any explanation derived from a prearranged structure, including that of "the double in fiction," results in similar irrelevance. On the other hand, I believe a psychological reading of

input/output procedure of determinist thinking which he achieves with the image of the final form of Felix's sausage and pretzel. [7]

To return, then, from the intensity of the critic's desire to the intensity of Hermann's, it is revealing to note that Hermann has to make certain protestations that draw attention as much to the difference between him and Felix as to the similarity. In Chapter 1 he discusses their respective facial features, proving "his point, going on splendidly. You now see both of us, reader. Two, but with a single face" (D, 27). He could stop there, but he doesn't.

> Look nearer: I possess large yellowish teeth; his are whiter and set more closely together, but is that really important? On my forehead a vein stands out like a capital M imperfectly drawn, but when I sleep my brow is as smooth as that of my double. And those ears . . . the convolutions of his are but very slightly altered in comparison with mine: here more compressed, there smoothed out. We have eyes of the same shape, narrowly slit with sparse lashes, but his iris is paler than mine. (D, 27)

He mentions the eyes again, contradicting in the process his earlier observation: "Our eyes alone were not quite identical but what likeness did exist between them was a mere luxury; for his were closed as he lay on the ground before me, and though I have never really seen, only felt, my eyelids when shut, I know that they differed in nothing from his eye-eaves" (D, 39).

If one should add these "admissions" to the judgments of resemblance by the other observers who are less evasive, one

---

Golyadkin's splitting on the Ismailovsky Bridge would seem quite appropriate to Dostoevsky, but *Despair* bids, "Farewell, Dusty." And see both the discussion of possible titles for the novel (by Hermann, p. 211) and section II of this chapter.

7. When Hermann first meets Felix, he notes "a pretzel and the greater part of a sausage" in Felix's knapsack; the next day he revisits the scene and finds, among other things, "that pathetically impersonal trace which the unsophisticated wanderer is wont to leave under a bush: one large, straight, manly piece and a thinner one coiled over it" (D, 19 and 27).

should also note Hermann's crucial distinction between the eyes when open, and when closed. It is the latter condition he is concerned with: though at the time of the meeting he had no explicit plan for Felix, at the time of his writing he has already executed that plan, and with his resulting knowledge can indicate from the beginning that it is death he aims at. Thus, what Felix looks like asleep is more to the purpose than how he appears awake. "That man," says Hermann, "especially when he slept, when his features were motionless, showed me my own face, my mask, the flawlessly pure image of my corpse" (D, 25).

I think, however, that more than the planting of signposts is going on in such passages. Hermann is interested in death long before he finds Felix, and after that meeting he is interested in more than the death of just Felix. One reason that it is insufficient, which is to say exclusive, to attribute Hermann's desperation to the breakup of his marriage and his business is that the central characteristic of both those aspects of his life is also central to his use of Felix. The physical death of the creature becomes not an end in itself only, but another instance, metaphorical from a certain perspective, of Hermann's general desire for a particular kind of arrangement of life.

"Harmony" and "order" are the two terms that Hermann uses to articulate that arrangement on the occasions when he criticizes Lydia and his domestic life with her. She is, for example, "wretchedly untidy." "Her slovenliness showed in the very way she walked"; in her chest of drawers "there writhed higgledy-piggledy a farrago" of all sorts of objects, and "quite often, too, there would dribble into the cosmos of my beautifully arranged things some tiny and very dirty lace handkerchief or a solitary stocking, torn." In fine, "decidedly, she had not the faintest notion of the mysteries of harmony" (D, 35).

One has to realize the way the notion of "order" pervades

Hermann's life before he can accept a term like "cosmos" and a phrase like "mysteries of harmony" as aptly used in the discussion of a messy chest of drawers. The point is that Lydia's entire life is disorderly; the importance of that to Hermann should be a bit more resonant when one remembers his politics. To call him a Marxist is to grant him an inappropriate sense of academic intelligence, though he does say "Marxism get[s] the nearest to Absolute Truth" (D, 134). He is, though, an articulate sympathizer with the 1917 revolution in Russia, from which country he is an expatriate of sorts. He believes communism "in the long run . . . a great and necessary thing." Western minds are unable to comprehend the "wonderful values" of "new" Russia: "History had never yet known such enthusiasm, asceticism, and unselfishness, *such faith in the impending sameness of us all*" (D, 30, my italics). That is the basket of order and harmony into which Hermann places his eggs. He explains, "I have always believed that the mottled tangle of our elusive lives demands such essential change; that Communism shall indeed create a beautifully square world of identical brawny fellows, broad-shouldered and microcephalous; and that a hostile attitude toward it is both childish and preconceived."[8] Hermann not only takes a friendly attitude toward communism, he becomes an active agent for its realization. In this context, then, I think one is better able to see Hermann's preoccupation with Felix's face in repose: "Life only marred my double," he says (D, 25), echoing an earlier remark. On another occasion old age affords him an arresting tangent: "It

8. Page 30. It seems appropriate, though I hope unnecessary, to point out here how radically Hermann's position disagrees with his creator's. As Nabokov says in his Foreword (p. 7), Hermann will be frustrated in his hope that his book "may find a market in the U.S.S.R." under the "diaphanous spuriousness of your [*i.e.*, V.N.'s] signature" (D, 168). The effects on human beings of the "standardization" Hermann loves are devastatingly portrayed in *Bend Sinister* and *Invitation to a Beheading*, which, alas, poor Hermann could not read. To see how absolutely Nabokov has always condemned totalitarian governments and their police methods in particular, see *Strong Opinions*, especially pages 48, 113, 133, 149, and 156.

interested me hugely to observe how our remarkable likeness got broken by the working of his face. If he were to attain old age, I reflected, his grins and grimaces would end by eroding completely our resemblance which is now so perfect when his face freezes" (D,85).[9] Old age is not, as it turns out, a viable alternative for Felix, and Hermann treats himself to a final look at his "double's" face after he has shot him in the woods: "At that moment when all the required features were fixed and frozen, our likeness was such that really I could not say who had been killed, I or he" (D,182). I do not mind at all giving this an allegorical reading, seeing, indeed, that a man who not only believes in the "impending sameness of us all," but who acts as an agent for the particular kind of "essential change" for "the mottled tangle of our elusive lives" that Hermann does, is himself a dead man, and there *is* no difference between him and a corpse. Such a life is, in effect, both suicide and homicide.[10]

My allegorical focus, however, doesn't jibe with the one Hermann suggests:

> It even seems to me sometimes that my basic theme, the resemblance between two persons, has a profound allegorical meaning. This remarkable physical likeness probably appealed to me (subconsciously!) as the promise of that ideal sameness which is to unite people in the classless society of the future; and by striving to make use of an isolated case, I was, though still blind to social truths, fulfilling, nevertheless, a certain social function. (D,168)

Even though it is *post rem*, Hermann articulates here the con-

9. The Narcissus story is used, appropriately, in connection with these passages (see pages 23 and 182). The implications here, however, are radically opposite to those I have discussed in *The Real Life of Sebastian Knight*. Here no flower blooms.

10. Ardalion may not be dear to your heart, a bit soggy and perhaps something of a fraud himself—he locates the Sistine Chapel in Dresden and doesn't mind being labeled a "dauber" by his mistress—but in the context of the novel he "perceives differences" (D,51), which renders him morally superior, and aesthetically preferable, to the bloke he cuckolds.

junction of aims my argument has been lurching toward. There is one other aspect of the moral cost of being a true believer in doubles and doubling, and Hermann is articulate about that, too, though perhaps a trifle less self-conscious. His consideration of the "social function" of his act continues this way:

> And then there is something else; the fact of my not being wholly successful when putting that resemblance of ours to practical use can be explained away by purely social-economic causes, that is to say, by the fact that Felix and I belonged to different, sharply defined classes, the fusion of which none can hope to achieve single-handed, especially nowadays, when the conflict of classes has reached a stage where compromise is out of the question. (D, 169)

The "system" to which Felix allies the "allegorical explanation" of his deeds allows him, conveniently, to avoid taking responsibility for them. "Social-economic" is a phrase which reverberates with impersonal yet official sanction, a veritable echo chamber in whose ringing confines one may, as one's brain turns to jelly, absolve oneself of responsibility for *anything*, even being there. The use of such language is itself irresponsible, but in perfect keeping with the utopia that derives eventually from Hermann's fond fantasy: "a new world where all men will resemble one another as Hermann and Felix did; a world of Helixes and Fermanns; a world where the worker fallen dead at the feet of his machine will be replaced by his perfect double smiling the serene smile of perfect socialism" (D, 169).[11]

11. In presenting as I am the moral aspect of the parody of the double motif, it may well seem I have, while drawing away, tumbled backwards into another pit: the rest of the passage from which I have been quoting presents briefly alternative emphases that will be made by various nationalities of readers, making the "Soviet" reading but one possibility among many. The crucial difference, I believe, is that Hermann believes his propaganda, while the reader is to see it as profoundly inhuman, and reject it. The parody is not accomplished only through Hermann's belief; the reader's disbelief has to be added. A "Soviet" reader would miss the parody altogether, as would any of the national stereotypes who populate the paragraph with him.

Hermann's wish to sidle free of responsibility has its mildly poignant side, too. His conscience is alive enough to need appeasing, in however devious a way. For instance, after he has gotten the little girl playing marbles to mail his letter, he imagines her future as in part determined by her having acted as his intermediary. Whatever part fate will play in *her* life, Hermann says, "My conscience is clear. Not I wrote to Felix, but he wrote to me; not I sent him the answer, but an unknown child" (D,135). I would go so far as to add that Hermann's theory of art and crime (D,132–33), with its emphasis on the independent force of a "creative" plan set in motion carrying itself forward with inexorable logic toward its inevitable conclusion, is itself another form his seeking to be personally non-responsible takes. It partakes of the same machinelike perfection his vision of future society incorporates. Such a procedure is not programmed for self-evaluation or self-abortion; a human being, on the other hand, can choose at any time to abandon a given course of action.

Hermann *is*, of course, a machine of sorts: a character in a novel is no more a human being than is any equally sophisticated computer. His perfection, however, is not realized in the terms he envisions, but in terms of the purposes he is serving his creator. Hermann's mistake serves the novel's perfection; the consequences of his choices are such that one sees what it costs to believe in doubles, to take seriously the transference of one's self onto a supposed mirror image. I think that is reasonably evident in *Despair*, and I believe the novel acts as a hub from and toward which all double play in Nabokov's other novels radiates.

It is, however, less clear because not so thoroughly dramatized—Nabokov's narrators seldom sharing their author's concern with such matters—that the double motif is also aesthetically dissatisfying. Briefly put, it is too simple. The assumption, however modulated, behind all fiction in which a double appears, never itself questioned by writer *or* critic, is that man is dual. This is most blatant in Stevenson's tale; the assumption *precedes* the story, and precedes Jekyll's "Full Statement of the Case" with which it ends. Thus, even what is most arresting conceptually about *The Strange Case of Dr. Jekyll and Mr. Hyde*—the "trembling immateriality" of the body, the "natural body" as "mere aura and effulgence of certain of the powers that made up [the] spirit"—is not confronted because the limitation of the basic assumption doesn't admit it. The conception of man's dual nature is a tyrant, to say the least, perhaps because, like tyranny, it promises neatness.

Both Stevenson and Dostoevsky, in fact, suggest explicitly another possibility. Golyadkin's dream (Chapter 10) of uncountable Golyadkins springing like Cadmus' warriors from his own footsteps is at least more interesting (and I think truer) than the assumption that awake he can be adequately accounted for as a human being by being split in two. But having cracked the door, Dostoevsky fails to open it farther. Similarly, Stevenson has Jekyll "hazard the guess that man will be ultimately known for a mere polity of multifarious, incongruous and independent denizens," and then fails to develop that population. Perhaps the philters and drafts of the time were inadequate to such multiple release, one wonders, and then realizes that it wasn't Stevenson who quaffed them.

And what is it, to shift the focus slightly, that is responsible for our thinking (as who hasn't?) that what we see in the mirror can be somehow fundamentally different from what we live in on this side of it? That is an illusion profoundly more mysterious than the visual one on the silvered glass. For the image we see on that glass is exactly the same (to the eye) as the object that casts it, and promises repetition and reproduction, not an image onto which we may fasten our imperfections and be rid of them. What we have on this side, we would have there. Life in a mirror would be no less complex and various than it is outside of one, assuming the illusion would bear you.

The supremely difficult and therefore interesting conceptions are *one* and *many*; *two* is a cop-out, epistemologically, aesthetically, morally, as Hermann, to considerably more than his chagrin, discovers.

II   APRIL FOOL

As it happens, mirrors and the discussion of them are the means Nabokov uses to draw the reader to the edge of the parody. Hermann despises mirrors, as he tells us on his second day of composition in Pignan, and well he might by then, considering how thoroughly he has deceived himself through his fancied human reflection, Felix. Because he won't use a mirror anymore, he hasn't shaved since the murder, when he shaved his victim, and hides now "in the natural jungle that has grown out of me" (D,31). And yet, in the midst of expressing his loathing for the very sound *mirror* he suddenly calls his fear "silly superstition" and begins to repeat the word over and over.

Without exhausting the detail of the crucial passages (they run about four pages, beginning at the top of 31), I would note simply that the thread on which the gauds of Hermann's monologue clicker is not the subject of mirrors, or superstitions, but rather preoccupation with silly habits and pursuits in general, a more inclusive topic: he mentions Lydia's various medieval dream theories, for example, her use of national stereotypes, and her method of choosing a book at the library, which has nothing to do with the book's contents. It is in the context of this haphazard, hermetic, and pointless jumble of pastimes that the talk about mirrors is set, purposely, I think, to indicate how a preoccupation with reflection is to be evaluated. If, however, the reader misses the signals, or persists in spite of them in his concern with the precious motif of the double, Hermann has a capping move to make. He pushes the shiny side of the matter right up to the reader's face.

> Tum-tee-tum. And once more—TUM! No, I have not gone mad. I am merely producing gleeful little sounds. The kind of glee one experiences upon making an April fool of someone. And a damned good fool I *have* made of someone. Who is he? Gentle reader, look at yourself in the mirror, as you seem to like mirrors so much. (D, 34)

The last "entry" of the book is dated April 1st,[12] and it seems at least likely that one way to read the joke on the reader is in the general terms I've been using myself: he has bought the double act and now that the curtain is coming down he is the victim of his gullibility, or inattention, or stubbornness, or whatever.

But there are other possibilities confined more strictly to the passages I have been discussing. For example, just before his exposure of the April fool, Hermann has been recounting Lydia's intense involvement with a detective novel. Because she is tempted to peep at the last pages ahead of time, she "tore the book in two down its back and hid the second, concluding, portion" (D, 33). Lydia forgets where the hiding place is, and as she goes about the house searching for it she repeats, "It was so exciting, so terribly exciting; I know I shall die if I don't find out—." The succeeding paragraph is the most enigmatic in the novel. In it Hermann states that Lydia found out, and, as

---

12. It is these dates, of course, that key the brief parody of Joyce's *Portrait of the Artist as a Young Man*, which Nabokov has called "a feeble and garrulous book" (SO, 71). The purpose of this particular allusion may not be as readily obvious as, say, "Crime and Pun," but it seems to me as thematically revealing. Stephen Dedalus in Joyce's book takes himself with heavy seriousness, but his author seeks in multiple ways to distance him from the reader and prevent the reader from seeing him as a "hero" to be admired or emulated. As an "artist" he writes one poem and a diary entry or two. This fraudulence is echoed in Hermann's entire experience, as well as in the immediate juxtaposition of "April 1st" and his assertion that "the danger of my tale deteriorating into a lame diary is fortunately dispelled" (D,221). For the fullest development of this reading of Stephen Dedalus, see Stanley Sultan, *The Argument of Ulysses* (Columbus: Ohio State University Press, 1964).

convincingly, implies that she didn't. "The poor dead woman," he says.

Is Gentle Reader an April fool because he reads that lament literally—Lydia is dead, killed, perhaps, by haywire hubby?—missing the metaphorical syllogism—Lydia would die if she didn't find out, she didn't find out, ergo . . .? Or is it that Gentle Reader, himself impatient and highly susceptible to suggestion, has turned to the back of *this* novel to see if, indeed, Lydia has been done in? Both are considerable possibilities. There is another, however, that is even more intriguing.

The book Lydia severed from itself was a "rotten detective novel with a crimson spider amid a black web on its cover"; when Lydia wants the hidden portion and can't find it, she is "a long, long time searching the house for the criminal she herself had concealed."[13] Both passages reverberate with the novel we, gentle readers all, hold in our hands, ourselves "harboring" criminal Hermann for the nonce. I would be straining the passage unduly, however, if there were nothing more done with this particular implication. More is, and the creaking subsides. When Hermann outlines for Lydia his little plan (Chapter 8) their initial exchange goes:

> "His [Felix's] plan is as follows," I went on, in a bland voice: "My life, say, is insured for half a million. In a wood, somewhere, my corpse is found. My widow, that is you—"
>
> "Oh stop saying such horrors," cried Lydia, scrambling up from the carpet. "I've just been reading a story like that. Oh, do please stop—" (D, 151)

As the transmission clears and becomes smoother, Hermann proposes that Lydia "imagine all I'm telling you is fiction. Quite seriously, you know, I've been trying to make myself believe that it was purely an invention of mine or some story I

13. Lydia, in her insistence before she has seen it that Felix's body is Hermann's, can be said to conceal a criminal.

had read somewhere" (D, 151). Lydia interrupts him, and then he continues, "The hero of this cheap mystery story demands the following measures," which he lists, eliciting this response from Lydia, whose manner has altered markedly:

> "Oh, wait a bit... I've remembered something: he somehow fixed the revolver to the bridge... No, that's wrong: he first tied a stone with a string... let me see, how did it go? Oh, I've got it: he tied a big stone to one end and the revolver to the other, and then shot himself. And the stone fell in the water, and the string followed across the parapet, and the revolver came next—all splash into the water. Only I can't remember why it was necessary." (D, 154)

"Smooth water, in brief; and a dead man left on the bridge," Hermann counterpoints. The plan works out somewhat differently in certain details, but, given this later development of the connection of "our" novel with the one Lydia (and Hermann) has been reading, it seems plausible that, in addition to the other possibilities this ample rumination accommodates, Gentle Reader is an April fool because he fails to acknowledge the basic fictional nature of the experience he is involved in.

That particular focus—the danger of the reader substituting a book, however briefly, for his own life—is by now a predictable aspect of my general consideration of Nabokov's work. I don't think a detailed documentation of the other means by which this constant possibility is constantly thwarted in *Despair* is necessary. There are numerous false starts and abandonments of certain modes of storytelling in the opening chapter of the novel, misleading and inconclusive alternative narrative tactics in Chapter 3, two addresses by trapped Hermann to his potent and mobile author (who does not send *him* an acorn or a moth), and even a homey and indulgent fake ending (D, 185–90).

In *Despair* the farthest reach of this familiar landscape is the wordplay involving Hermann's fatal oversight. In terms of this geographical metaphor one might ask, with some appropriateness, *Is the world really flat? Will I fall off?*—to which the answers are, *yes,* and *yes again, but only if you have been fooled into thinking it's round.* If the joke of the motif of the double has worked—*i.e.*, if one has been taken in by it—then he could possibly get a large and anticlimactic jolt when the "shaggy dog" conclusion hits him (*if* it does). It would be a matter of how far Gentle Reader falls out of the book, which is to say, off the edge of the cornered world. The pun, as usual in the case of such jokes, is mean: Hermann failed because he missed a made stick. For the reader who has not been duped, there is no problem, no letdown, because he has scaled no false height to begin with, and has been tipped off quite early anyhow, as I have already pointed put.

One avoids the temptation to dismiss *Despair* as a long way to go for a clever phrase, when one considers the importance of both the manner of conveyance and the particular angles of vision it affords the traveler. One receives not only a delightful parody of a much-practiced mode of literary perception, but some valuable suggestions—dramatic, composite, reticulate —about the way such perception can issue in consequences of a perilous kind.

SIX

Floating
and Singing:
The Novel
as Biography

I APPROACHING THE NARRATOR

It is possible to consider all of Nabokov's novels, as, to some degree, revealing the fiction of biography, and at least one of them, *Ada*, as a biography of fiction. *The Real Life of Sebastian Knight* has been written about from the former perspective,[1] and I think it is rewarding to think of *Pnin*, his twelfth novel and his fourth in English, in the same way.

The general implications of the novel, read from this angle, are similar to those of most of Nabokov's work. As in the books I have already considered, one moves finally into the shifting ambience of parody, and what is parodied turns out to be not so much a literary form used by other writers as more basic assumptions about perception and its relationship to so-called factual reality, that term which Nabokov has frequently said should be surrounded by quotation marks. In this instance, however, the particular form that is used to intensify those marks is more immediately and unquestioningly associated

1. By Susan Fromberg, convincingly, in "The Unwritten Chapters in *The Real Life of Sebastian Knight*," *Modern Fiction Studies*, XIII (Winter, 1967), 427-42.

with *facts* than, for instance, is a detective story, the cinema, or a play. One picks up a biography expecting automatically *not* to encounter fiction, but to be presented with an objective account of a life. And I suspect that even when one has read two or three biographies of the same person, which is to say two or three versions of a "reality" (or two or three realities), he still has trouble relinquishing his illusion that there is a factual base, which he can piece together, underlying the various ornamentations of it. That piecing together would, of course, be nothing more than another version, another biography; such a process of interlocking and superimposing versions has, in fact, been at the core of *The Real Life of Sebastian Knight*, and recurs, more subtly, in *Pnin*.

Unlike the earlier novel, *Pnin* is structured so that very few signals of its parodic nature occur; one has to wait until the last chapter of the novel to be sure that his illusions have been monkeyed with, for it is not until then that the suspicious relationship of the narrator with his subject becomes explicit. There is in *Pnin* no acknowledgment of the process of accumulating data—nobody is visiting the friends of a dead person, trying to organize the bits and pieces he picks up into a unified whole. One is presented the whole to begin with, or so it appears, and the tendency to settle comfortably into the easy chair of reportage is encouraged. It takes a while for the needle in the cushion to work its way into the flesh.

The methods of encouragement are familiar to biography—and emphasis on names, places, dates. Almost all of the characters who appear in *Pnin*, no matter how minor they seem, are given names: the students who enroll in Pnin's Russian language classes, the expatriates who gather in the summers at Al Cook's, even Judith Clyde at Cremona College and Grigoriy Belochkin, who may or may not have turned over a glass of pear *kvas* at a famous resort on the Baltic coast. The only important character who goes nameless is, strikingly, the narrator, but it is possible, as I will argue later, that the whole novel is in the process of naming him.

Places are handled with the same care, giving the same impression of local identity. Waindellville is, in effect, on a map; after a chapter or so that map becomes partly familiar, for it includes Albany and is clearly of an upstate New York and New England area. Victor's trip to visit Pnin is presented in such a way as to underline this, giving us another "real" city, Boston (to which Framingham is adjacent), by which the reader can orient himself. This is carried to something of a finite extreme by the narrator's aerial perspective on Pnin's highway and dirtway vicissitudes on his way to Cook's.

The novel abounds with dates as well: Pnin's series of "heart attacks," beginning on July 4, 1920; his birthdays, two of which are central events in the novel; the recurrent reminders of how long he has been at Waindell; the temporal exactness of occurrences from his past. Overriding these specific instances is the concern with chronology, beginning first with the specification of the year, and eventually of the seasons within the year, and the time of day.

Name, place, date, the chronology of events. It is no wonder one believes he is reading the true story of Timofey Pnin, presented objectively, if with sympathy, by someone who has the inside information, who is trustworthy, and who has no stake in what he is writing, no axe to grind.

But even without the final chapter, it would be surprising if a reader of this novel could get very far with that belief, for Nabokov gives hints that the case is otherwise—gives them gently, and with reserve, but tellingly nonetheless. To begin, for instance, where the novel begins—with the narrative perspective, *not* with Pnin—one sees the gentlest of these suggestions right away. After Pnin's appearance has been described in the novel's first two paragraphs, the narrator remarks, "Thus he might have appeared to a fellow passenger;

but except for a soldier asleep at one end and the two women absorbed in a baby at the other, Pnin had the coach to himself."[2] The conditional is suggestive—he *might* have appeared thus to someone else, but then again he might not—but what is more interesting is the question of who is seeing Pnin if no one on the train has paid him any attention. This sentence is followed immediately by the narrator's imparting of the "secret" known to no one in the coach, including Pnin himself: Pnin is on the wrong train. The only person who can be both observing and knowing is the narrator; as soon as the novel begins Nabokov is, as always, making his preparations carefully. Further, it is no slip on the author's part that the narrator speaks of the distance between Waindell and Cremona in terms of versts instead of miles, and we learn in this same chapter that the narrator had assisted Pnin in writing to the New York *Times* in 1945; he begins to show as well his habit of referring to Pnin as "my friend," which one learns later is something of a liberty.

This process of suggestion, designed to undermine the reader's belief in the detachment of the narrator and therefore in the appearance of a factual account of Pnin's life, continues, becoming a little more obvious with each of the next five chapters, and, predictably, more complex in its implications. The narrator's involvement in Pnin's past shows more sharply, for instance, when he reveals that a relative of his helped with Pnin's emigration from Europe in 1939, and the reader might begin to wonder what the narrator is holding back when he refers to Pnin's love letter to Liza, in which Pnin proposed to her, as "now safe in a private collection" (P, 45). His reference to the "litterateur" with whom Liza had an affair, as a result of which she attempted suicide, has the same effect.

2. *Pnin* (Garden City, N.Y.: Doubleday & Company, 1957), 8. All subsequent quotations are from this edition, and are followed by page numbers in parentheses.

His pronunciation of "Tsentral Park and Reeverside" (P,62), which are echoes of Pnin's pronunciation, intensify one's sense that he is Russian himself. Once the novel reaches the way station of Al Cook's rambling country house one is certain; the narrator sheds the appearance of emotional distance he has more or less been trying to sustain, as his comments on Cook's childless marriage illustrate.

Moreover, in these chapters (2 through 6) the narrator continues to "report" Pnin's activities so as to extend the suggestiveness of his opening observations. He goes where Pnin goes, and because of this Pnin is never alone, even when he dreams.[3] Two particular passages may be to the point of the general technique here. The first is the closing paragraph of Chapter 4: "Presently all were asleep again. It was a pity nobody saw the display in the empty street, where the auroral breeze wrinkled a large luminous puddle, making of the telephone wires reflected in it illegible lines of black zigzags" (P,110). Somebody *does* see it, however, and gives it to the reader as though it were a perception no different from the other perceptions in the book. More extensive an example occurs in the opening five pages of Chapter 5. The narrator presents Pnin's search for Cook's house from the perspective of a fire tower overlooking the countryside. His observation is set in the same negative mode as the opening description of Pnin on the train, and the sight of the puddle I have just referred to. It is *as if* no one was there to see.

> [Pnin's] various indecisions and gropings took those bizarre visual forms that an observer . . . might have followed with a compassionate eye; but there was no living creature in that forlorn and listless upper region except for an ant who had his own

---

3. One might refer to the narrative tension I am discussing here, in more traditional terms, as the first-person point of view masquerading as the third. The guide who tightly squeezes one's hand tries, at the same time, to seem invisible.

> troubles, having, after hours of inept perseverance, somehow
> reached the upper platform and the balustrade. (P, 115)

But again, it *is* seen; the narrator, in fact, follows that ant to
the "right beam leading to the roof of the tower," and tells his
auditor the names visitors have penciled on the balustrade of
the tower. The details of each of these scenes are given and
taken away at the same time, but nonetheless they are *seen*,[4]
and the basic effect of the *way* they are seen is to make one
aware that the narrative intelligence of the novel is working in
a mode fundamentally different from the usual mode the biog-
rapher assumes. If one becomes aware of the imaginative nature of such scenes he should begin to question the nature of
other details which are not *apparently* surrounded by an
aura of invention.

To the narrator's involvement in Pnin's past, the indication
that he is withholding information, and his ability to see and
know things no one else, including Pnin, sees or knows,
Nabokov adds another method that serves to alert his reader to
the fictional nature of this apparent biography. He has the narrator at least twice comment on the narration, a tactic, as I
have indicated in other connections, that is familiar in his
novels and is, in fact, used more sparingly here than elsewhere. In Chapter 1 he notes:

> Some people—and I am one of them—hate happy ends. We
> feel cheated. Harm is the norm. Doom should not jam. The
> avalanche stopping in its tracks a few feet above the cowering
> village behaves not only unnaturally but unethically. Had I
> been reading about this mild old man instead of writing about
> him, I would have preferred him to discover, upon his arrival to
> Cremona, that his lecture was not this Friday but the next.
> (P, 25–6)

And in Chapter 2, after the Waindell bells have been

4. William W. Rowe finds such giving and taking away a Gogolian trait, which
he discusses in other contexts, and in more detail, in *Nabokov's Deceptive World* (New
York: New York University Press, 1972).

modulated into the ringing telephone in the Clement's house, he says,

> Technically speaking, the narrator's art of integrating telephone conversations still lags far behind that of rendering dialogues conducted from room to room, or from window to window across some narrow blue alley in an ancient town with water so precious, and the misery of donkeys, and rugs for sale, and minarets, and foreigners and melons, and the vibrant morning echoes. (P,31)

In themselves these passages should at least alert the reader that he is in the presence of fiction, as well as the presence of the intelligence creating it. But it should do a little more. The details used—the avalanche, the windows and the alley, the donkey, rugs and minarets—should, by their inappropriateness in this novel, suggest, through their own romantic and fantastic (to an American reader) qualities, that perhaps, *mutatis mutandis*, basically everything that surrounds them is just as inappropriate in the larger arena of apparent factual reality. The kind of extrapolation these details suggest is similar to the one carried a bit farther in "The Murder of Gonzago" in *Hamlet*: here is a play presented by traveling players: here are other players— Gertrude, Hamlet, etc.—watching the play; here are other people (the audience, or also players?) watching the players watching the players. And who is watching them? Likewise, reading *Pnin* is not simply a matter of noticing consciously that one is reading fiction, but that its deceptive appearance as reported fact is not limited to this book, or even to the act of reading.

As I have said, all this is suggestive until Chapter 7. At that point a good deal becomes explicit and the pattern of earlier hint and evocation is fulfilled. The narrator openly acknowledges his relationship with Pnin, finding its beginning in 1911 when he had a mote removed from his eye by Pnin's father.[5]

5. This rather fatuously implies that the narrator is to be compared with Tolstoy at least, and possibly Dostoevsky. See the references to these two writers, and Dr. Pavil Pnin, on pages 21 and 26 of the novel.

He recounts later meetings with Pnin, in Paris, and New York, and reveals much of what he has teasingly withheld previously. The "private collection" in which Pnin's letter of proposal to Liza resides is the narrator's (P, 182), and he quotes the letter. The "littérateur" with whom Liza had the nearly fatal affair is the narrator, of course (P, 180–82); it is he, finally, who is the "fascinating lecturer" who takes Pnin's place at Waindell. The reference made in Chapter 5 to Mira and "amateur theatricals" (P. 133) is expanded in more detail (P, 177–79), as is the role of the Baltic resort in Pnin's adolescence. It is even possible that Victor's art teacher, Lake, who has "studied in Paris" and whose decision to "bury himself" in an anonymous New England boy's school puzzles those who recognize his genius, has also had an affair with Victor's mother, for in that letter of proposal Pnin refers to "the celebrated painter who made your portrait last year [who] is now... drinking himself to death... in the wilds of Massachusetts" (P, 183).

This much, I think, is easy, and could be set aside as another instance of the little games played with the reader's expectations that gives in the end a pleasure similar to the kind solving a puzzle affords, and as easily forgotten. But, as I have shown to be the case elsewhere, what seems in a Nabokov novel to be an answer, or a solution, is rather the ground for a more illuminating mystery. He conceals the keys of his patterns so that one considers him kin to the designer Pnin's narrator refers to as "the destroyer of minds, the friend of fever" (P, 23).

In Chapter 7 the reader is led beyond all the clarifications he receives. The narrator's language, first of all, is revealing in places. For example:

> Perhaps because on my visits to schoolmates I had seen other middle-class apartments, I *unconsciously* retained a picture of the Pnin flat that *probably* corresponds to reality. I can *report*

> therefore that *as likely as not* it consisted of two rows of rooms
> divided by a long corridor; on one side was the waiting room,
> the doctor's office, *presumably* a dining room and a drawing
> room further on. (P, 176, my italics)

The clarification of details from Pnin's (and the narrator's) life
in this chapter may, after all, simply confirm the reader's sense
that all is well, that the little game of coy obfuscation still results in the reporting of facts. But a passage such as this makes
that conclusion impossible; one wonders how much else that
has been "reported" is presumption and probability. Moreover, that this is so is intensified by Pnin's denial of the narrator's presentation of some details of his past.

> I tried not only to remind Pnin of former meetings, but also to
> amuse him and other people around us with the unusual lucid-
> ity and strength of my memory. However, he denied every-
> thing. He said he vaguely recalled my grandaunt but had never
> met me. He said that his marks in algebra had always been poor
> and that, anyway, his father had never displayed him to pa-
> tients. . . . He repeated that we had never seen each other be-
> fore. (P, 180)

With that we should be sure that what we have been reading is
invention, an imaginative construction, a fiction partly disguised as fact. But again I think one could live with this comfortably, by putting it aside as part of a book, intriguing but
merely literary. The final dimension toward which this process
moves, and in which it is left to reside, is, however, much
more disturbing, and though it can be spoken of as though it is
understood it remains impossible to explain away.

The novel stops, but does not conclude, with this passage:

> Cockerell, brown-robed and sandaled, let in the cocker and led
> me kitchenward, to a British breakfast of depressing kidney and
> fish.
> "And now," he said, "I am going to tell you the story of Pnin
> rising to address the Cremona Women's Club and discovering
> he had brought the wrong lecture."

The novel has opened with an account of Pnin's trip to deliver a lecture to the Cremona Women's Club, but in that account he has forestalled getting caught with the wrong lecture by intricate precautions, and eventually by getting off a bus and recovering the "right" lecture at the bus station where he had left it. The final passage of the novel seems to take us back to its beginning, as though in a circle, but in reality it takes us back to a point *analogous* to the beginning but *not* identical with it. The figure of a spiral would perhaps be more accurate a metaphor for the movement involved. Back to the lecture and the trip, but with a different emphasis, or in a different version. We have seen this event once; if Mr. Cockerell, who lets in his cocker, were to deliver his account we would see it again, but changed.

Cockerell has, in fact, used up the narrator's evening and early morning before this breakfast with an exhausting series of imitations of Pnin, done so well that the narrator is forced to wonder "if by some poetical vengeance this Pnin business had not become with Cockerell the kind of fatal obsession which substitutes its own victim for that of the initial ridicule" (P, 189). The particular events that Cockerell has recounted during his imitations have, with only a few expectations, already been presented to us by the narrator during the course of his book-length imitation of Pnin: "Pnin teaching, Pnin eating, Pnin ogling a coed.... We got Pnin in the Stacks, and Pnin on the Campus Lake. We heard Pnin criticize the various rooms he had successively rented" (P, 187). It is not stretching things to imagine the evening with Cockerell as another novel called *Pnin*, presented via synopsis, created by a man with an obsession who has "acquired an unmistakable resemblance to the man he had now been mimicking for almost ten years" (P, 187).

These last two sections of the novel, then, open, suddenly, questions of a queasy sort, especially if one happens to be a person to whom facts and the assumption that facts are immutable are important. Who is Pnin? The one we have been accepting for 180 pages or so has gradually been revealed as the narrator's invention. We are given still another invention by Cockerell. There seems, indeed, to have been a walking, talking, teaching, eating, ogling, person called "Pnin" whom characters other than the narrator and Cockerell have seen and talked with and consoled and manipulated, but is he possibly only a convenience? Does he have any identity beyond the imitations we have been asked to accept as the man behind them? Is he an occasion by means of which others can identify themselves?

In the midst of such questions one might notice the degree to which twins are important in the novel. There is a set, Igor and Olga Poroshin, who appear, to disappear, at Cook's. The gas station attendant who gives Pnin directions is called "false Hagen," and Laurence Clements and Dr. Eric Wind briefly merge in Pnin's mind during his party. Pnin takes a book back to the library for the person who has requested it, who turns out to be himself, something more than absent-mindedness. There is the long diversion on Tristram Thomas and Thomas Wynn, Twinn and Winn, Tvin and Vin, that is carried through Pnin's inviting one while he thinks he is inviting the other to his party. Such twinning is said to be, by the narrator, common in academic communities, and he adds, "I know, indeed, of a case of triplets at a comparatively small college where, according to its sharp-eyed president, Frank Reade, the radix of the troika was, absurdly, myself" (P, 148). Not, assuredly, Waindell College, whose president is named Poore—assuredly, until we think of Timofey, Cockerell, and the narrator. But of course Pnin and the narrator have not been at Waindell at the same time. Or have they? The shadowy play of twinning upon the surface of the novel is taken into the same dimension the last passages lead us toward when Clements says to Thomas, "'He probably mistook you for somebody else, and for all I know you *may* be somebody else'" (P, 165). This is reminiscent of the conclusion of *Sebastian Knight*, but it is not so conclusive here.

There are, in fact, no explicit conclusions in *Pnin* to compare with Sebastian's half-brother's ability to say "I am Sebastian Knight, or he is I, or we are both someone neither of us knows." The narrator of *Pnin* may be no less ambiguous than "V", but he is less explicit, and I believe the novel itself is less explicit, too, probably the least explicit, most gently subtle, of all Nabokov's work. For the time being I will leave the possibilities which the questions I have raised indicate, and return to them in part III. Suffice it at this point to say that the presence of these possibilities makes it impossible to cling to the rock of fact, the settled comfort of biography; the book moves where all perception moves, in the imagination, where composition of realities takes place, and beyond which one puts reality in quotation marks. The nature of the composition can be approached, as I have been doing, as focusing on the relationship between form and perception, but it can also be approached from another direction.

II   RECURRENCE: EXILE

During the later stages of Pnin's party the reader is allowed to overhear a segment of Joan Clement's conversation: "'But don't you think—haw—that what he is trying to do—haw—practically in all his novels—haw—is—haw—to express the fantastic recurrence of certain situations?'" (P, 159). The reaction of anyone acquainted with Nabokov's work is to take him to be the antecedent of Mrs. Clement's pronouns, and, indeed, immediately following her comment one of those recurrences takes place. It is a simple one, not very fantastic, but it is set where it is to key the relevance of the statement to the novel in which it appears. Laurence Clements tells an off-color joke, to which Pnin responds, "I have heard quite the same anecdote thirty-five years ago in Odessa, and even then I could not understand what is comical in it" (P, 160). What is briefly suggested here turns out to be threaded into the fabric of the whole novel, most noticeably in Pnin's unpredictable (or predictable) recollections of his own past.[6] A number of these occur, and are handled so that they seem to be not simply recollection, but instances of the recurrence of events and people from a supposedly dead time. Nabokov's method seems, in fact, to be similar to Proust's use of the uneven flagstones, the napkin, the knocking pipe and, of course, the *petite madeleine*.

Just before he begins to deliver his lecture to the Cremona Women's Club, Pnin's audience is transformed:

> In the middle of the front row of seats he saw one of his Baltic aunts. . . . Next to her, shyly smiling, sleek dark head inclined, gentle brown gaze shining up at Pnin from under velvet eyebrows, sat a dead sweetheart of his. . . . Vanya Bednyashkin, shot by the Reds in 1919 in Odessa [the place and year Pnin heard Clements' joke] . . . was gaily signaling to his former schoolmate. . . . And in an inconspicuous situation Dr. Pavel Pnin and his anxious wife, both a little blurred but on the whole wonderfully recovered from their obscure dissolution, looked at their son with the same life-consuming passion and pride that they had looked at him with that night in 1912 when, at a school festival, commemorating Napolean's defeat, he had recited . . . a poem by Pushkin. (P, 27–28)

Similar recollections occur again, though the contexts afford-

---

6. During the following discussion I will, most of the time, accept the convenience of Pnin as a character who in some way has an existence of his own, apart from the narrator's imitation of him. That convenience, as I have tried to suggest, is *part* of the identity named "Pnin"; it is a manner of speaking. The novel is, of course, finally the narrator's embroilment, and to him the convenience of Pnin as a man apart from himself is of crucial importance. I will return to this focus in my conclusion.

ing the impetus for them change, in each chapter of the novel except the last. Sometimes the recurrence is treated, as here, in some detail: his transformation of Cook's summer house and its guests, for example, in which his father plays chess with Dr. Belochkin, and he meets Mira for the last time (P, 132–36). On other occasions it is briefly presented: while he is leafing through a Russian-language periodical in the library, he sees, "for no special reason," his father and mother relaxing in a drawing room in St Petersburg in 1913 (P, 75–76); on his way home from the Starr's "Russian" evening, and as he drifts off to sleep, he walks a Russian countryside, along a road that emerges into "the romantic, free, beloved radiance of a great field unmowed by time" (P, 82); at the gas station on the way to Cook's he becomes a Petrograd freshman again (P, 114) and recalls that instance once more a bit later (P, 124); his own rooms in the first house he rents remind him of Russian country houses (P, 146). The most significant constant in these instances is the time period which recurs; in each case it is *before* the 1918/19 revolutionary period. I will come back to this later in the context of Pnin's "illness" and his research.

Perhaps memory, even when it is treated in such a way as to shade it toward the past's recurrence, is not quite fantastic enough a mode, however, since we have invented psychological tools by means of which we think the fantasy can be removed. I don't think so, but perhaps. In view of the *perhaps*, it becomes somewhat important that Nabokov has used more than one means to make recurrence part of the experience of the book. The usual label for the following instances is "coincidence," a good term both because it explains nothing and because its primary meaning is in keeping with the purport of the novel. Chapter 4, which deals wholly with the second excruciatingly poignant visit Pnin has from a loved one, this time Victor, opens and closes suggestively. Victor dreams of his father as a king in the midst of a revolution that threatens his throne and his life.[7] He envisions the king as responding decisively to the situation, choosing to escape, by water. Victor never brings his vision to a conclusion, however, never gets the king his father to the beach and into the delivering motorboat, because, "the very act of postponing that thrilling and soothing episode, the very protraction of its lure, coming as it did on top of the repetitive fancy, formed the main mechanism of its soporific effect" (P,86). The closing scene involves Pnin's dream as he sleeps at the end of the evening he has spent with Victor: "Pnin saw himself fantastically cloaked, fleeing through great pools of ink under a cloud-barred moon from a chimerical palace, and then pacing a desolate strand with his dead friend . . . Polyanski as they waited for some mysterious deliverance to arrive in a throbbing boat from beyond the hopeless sea" (P, 109–110).

The dreams of "father" and "son" coincide; one completes the other, and the footprints which approach Pnin and cause him to wake up may belong to the friend of fever. This is difficult to see as anything but fantastic, and the agent of the fantasy signals his presence.

This instance of recurrence, or coincidence, involves Pnin and Victor, exiles from home and from each other; as such it is resonant with the recollections I have discussed. But people other than Pnin and his immediate "family" are included in this pattern. The "Russian revelers" whom Entwistle fooled into thinking he was a compatriot (P,36), for example, may have been the group at the champagne party cooked up to

7. Not surprisingly, the fantastic recurrence involves other Nabokov novels: of this particular instance Nabokov said in an interview (1966), "The boy at St. Mark's and Pnin both dream of a passage from my drafts of *Pale Fire*, the revolution in Zembla and the escape of the king—that is telepathy for you!" (SO,84). And, truncated but still recognizable, from *Laughter in the Dark* appears "a very gracious old lady, Dorianna Karen, famous movie star of the 20's" (D,159).

bribe "an influential critic. . . to devote his next *feuilleton* in one of the Russian-language newspapers to an appreciation of Liza's muse" (P,45). Both incidents take (or took) place at the Ougolok ("little corner") cafe in Paris. Or consider Jan van Eyck's "ample-jowled, fluff-haloed Canon van der Paele" to whom Laurence Clements bears a striking resemblance, as the narrator observes (P, 154). At the point of the observation Clements is holding an English-Russian, Russian-English dictionary in his hand, a book he puts aside later in favor of a volume titled *Flemish Masterpieces*, in which he finds himself, or rather Canon van der Paele. The unusual situation is more resonant still: the volume of reproductions has been given to Victor by his mother, and in turn left by its owner with Pnin; Victor is a budding artistic genius whose pursuits are spoken of this way:

> If Degas could immortalize a *caleche*, why could not Victor Wind do the same to a motor car?
> One way to do it might be by making the scenery penetrate the automobile. A polished black sedan was a good subject. . . . Break the body of the car into separate curves and panels; then put it together in terms of reflections. . . . In the chrome plating, in the glass of a sun-rimmed headlamp, he would see a view of the street and himself comparable to the microcosmic version of a room (with a dorsal view of diminutive people) in that very special and very magical small convex mirror that, half a millenium ago, Van Eyck and Petrus Christus and Memling used to paint into their detailed interiors. (P,96–98)

Again there is coincidence; this time the artistic locus is explicit, and the detail of the mirror serves to intensify the reflection of one experience in another. Finally, note that two pairs of characters who appear briefly have names which are nearly interchangeable: Christopher and Louise Starr, colleagues of Pnin's at Waindell, and Christine and Louis Stern, psychologists who test Victor. This connection is compounded later when we learn a few details of Liza's attempted suicide in the early twenties. Who saved her life? Why those two obliging English neighbors of hers, Chris and Lew.[8]

I think, further, that the instances of twinning which I have discussed in another context also bear on the theme of fantastic recurrence. Clements' statement to Thomas, "And for all I know you *may* be somebody else," may be considered in conjunction. with a comment the narrator makes about Pnin, some thirty pages earlier, immediately after the longest single instance of recollection in the novel: "The sky was dying. He did not believe in an autocratic God. He did believe, dimly, in a democracy of ghosts. The souls of the dead, perhaps, formed committees, and these, in continuous session, attended to the destinies of the quick" (P,136).

However, the most important details which have to do with the imaginative composition of realities in the novel come with the complexly associative descriptions of Pnin's "attacks" and his research, which are both connected in the figure of the squirrel.

Timofey has two "attacks" in the novel. Even if the narrator, his "physician for the nonce," did not register his doubt that the seizures are heart attacks, the manner of their presentation would lead one to doubt it. No doctor has been able to understand them in the past; Pnin has had four prior to the first one in the novel, which occurs just after he has left the bus in Whitchurch. This one, the first the reader encounters, defies a medical explanation, too. It is characterized by a sense of the divestment of the flesh, which is death, by a "tingle of unreality," and by a sense of becoming one with one's surroundings. It is both frightening and attractive, as occurrences that approach the miraculous tend to be: "It may be wonderful to mix with the landscape, but to do so is the end of the tender ego"

8. Another such instance involves Robert Karlovich Horn, a steward of the narrator's aunt's estate (and another castoff from the 1936 *Laughter in the Dark*) who "recurs" as Bob Horn, the bus station attendant who assists Pnin on his way to Cremona.

(P,20).[9] Yet the end of the tender ego we know may be the beginning of a tougher, more enduring one. The effect of this experience in Whitchurch on Pnin is to dislocate his ego from time: during the course of it he is both seated on the stone bench in the strange park in 1950 and lying in his bed with a fever in his home in St. Petersburg in 1910. There appear in the park rhododendrons and oaks; the same vegetation is pictured on the wallpaper of his room. On the polished wood screen near his bed are a path, an old man hunched on a bench, and a squirrel; he has walked down a path to the stone bench he is now (now?) hunched on, and when he comes out of his seizure his first sight is a squirrel on the ground before him.

He is, moreover, referred to as "a poor cocooned pupa" in the context of his childhood illness, but the context of the seizure makes that situation merge with the present so that the image applies to him on the bench as well.[10] A cocooned pupa is in a stage of transformation, as we know; in that condition Pnin looks at the wallpaper of his room (and the landscape of the park) and thinks that, "if the evil designer—the destroyer

9. Such dissolution is part of the Nabokov skyline. In *The Gift*, for instance, Fyodor Godunov-Cherdyntsev speaks of the effects of sunbathing on him: "I gradually felt I was becoming moltenly transparent, that I was permeated with flame and existed only insofar as it did. As a book is translated into an exotic idiom, so was I translated into sun"; after further lovely sylvan detail he concludes, "One might dissolve completely that way" (G,316). And Professor Adam Krug, talking to himself in partial parody of a lecture, says, "And now, ladies and gentlemen, we come to the problem of death. It may be said with a fair amount of truth as is practically available that to seek perfect knowledge is the attempt of a point in space and time to identify itself with every other point; death is either the instantaneous gaining of perfect knowledge (similar say to the instantaneous disintegration of stone and ivy composing the circular dungeon where formerly the prisoner had to content himself with only two small apertures optically fusing into one; whilst now, with the disappearance of all walls, he can survey the entire circular landscape), or absolute nothingness, *nichto*" (BS,174).

10. Just before Godunov-Cherdyntsev's "translation," an "Angle Wing butterfly with a white bracket on its dark mottled underside, suddenly . . . alighted on [his] bare chest, attracted by human sweat" (G,314). I think the magnetic quality of sweat an insufficient reason for the attraction here.

of minds, the friend of fever—had concealed the key of the pattern with such monstrous care, that key must be as precious as life itself and, when found, would regain for Timofey Pnin his everyday health, his everyday world" (P, 24). The passage, and the experience of which it is a part, are magnificent. In the superimposed temporal foci resides the dual significance of the illnesses: in 1910 Timofey recovered from his fever and regained his everyday health and his everyday world, and yet 1910 is inseparable from 1950: the Timofey of one time is also the Timofey of the other: he is still "ill" and still looking for that key. His everyday health and world are what he is exiled from: prerevolutionary Russia, the self that took that time and place as home and still retains it, fragmented and elusive, in the imagination. The self named Pnin has been composed narratively as fluid, as having versions, because that self, though it appears in particular places at specified times, is finally both placeless and timeless, a floating possibility that has nowhere to rest—except, perhaps, in some dimension we have no terms to realize, a dimension suggested by the image of the cocooned pupa,[11] and to which we make ourselves available through continuous imaginative composition, keeping alive and touching what seems to have been irrevocably lost.

Note how this circles about within the book. Pnin discusses

11. The manner in which Pnin's exit is handled in the next to last paragraph of the novel, and Lake's color theory seem to be other ways in which such a dimension is suggested. As Timofey passes the beer truck and disappears into the distance, the narrator ventures to say, "There was simply no saying what miracle might happen" (P,191). And "among the many exhilarating things Lake taught was that the order of the solar spectrum is not a closed circle but a spiral of tints from cadmium red and oranges through a strontium yellow and a pale paradisal green to cobalt blues and violets, at which point the sequence does not grade into red again but passes into another spiral, which starts with a kind of lavendar gray and goes on to Cinderella shades transcending human perception" (P,96). Because of passages such as these I have used the spiral as a figure for the form of the narration itself. See also my discussion of ecstasy in Chapter Seven.

his "condition" with his old friend Chateau prior to his swim at Cook's. Chateau reveals that he must have an operation in the near future, to which Pnin responds, "laughing, that every time *he* was X-rayed, doctors vainly tried to puzzle out what they termed 'a shadow behind the heart'" (P,126). A bit later Chateau cautions Pnin that he will someday lose the Greek Catholic cross he wears on a chain about his neck. "'Perhaps I would not mind losing it,' said Pnin. 'As you well know, I wear it merely from sentimental reasons. And the sentiment is becoming burdensome. After all, there is too much of the physical about this attempt to keep a particle of one's childhood in contact with one's breastbone'" (P, 128). The breastbone, the heart, the shadow behind, one's childhood—the combination of details extends the suggestions implicit in the first seizure.

Further, Pnin goes swimming immediately after these exchanges, which perhaps is a reminder that he has been characterized as Victor's "water father" by Eric Wind. Water is almost always associated with emigration in the novel, the "actual" one across the Atlantic by the whole "family" being the central instance. The vision which Victor conjures to make him sleep, which is completed in Pnin's dream, bears upon this theme too, for there the mode of escape from death at the hands of revolutionaries is water. As I have suggested, this is a more complex kind of recurrence; later I will return from another point on the circle to both the water imagery and Pnin's sense of burdensomeness.

The second "attack" he experiences in the novel occurs at Al Cook's. Its symptoms are the same as those of the first: "It was not pain or palpitation, but rather an awful feeling of sinking and melting into one's surroundings" (P,131). As in the previous occurrence, the details of his surroundings in the year of the seizure, 1954, are reflections of those of a past period, 1916 (or 1917): Cook's country house and the people visiting it coincide with the country house rented by Dr. Pavel Pnin's chess opponent, Yakov Belochkin, and the other people visiting there. The two scenes merge, as did the two scenes (and times) of the first seizure, this time accompanied by comment that makes the basic implications of Pnin's physical condition even clearer: "Pnin, with hallucinatory sharpness, imagined Mira slipping out there into the garden and coming toward him among tall tobacco flowers whose dull white mingled in the dark with that of her frock. *This feeling coincided somehow with the sense of diffusion and dilation within his chest*" (P,133, my italics). An additional focus appears, however, in the closing long passage of this attack. Mira died in a Nazi concentration camp, Buchenwald; the precise way she died is unknown, which means for Pnin that she continues to die in his imagination, over and over: "Mira kept dying a great number of deaths in one's mind, and undergoing a great number of resurrections, only to die again and again, led away by a trained nurse, inoculated with filth, tetanus bacilli, broken glass, gassed in a sham shower bath with prussic acid, burned alive in a pit on a gasoline-soaked pile of beechwood" (P,135). This should be intolerable to a human being, and for the most part Pnin exists by not thinking about it. It is only during his seizures that he is able even to begin to deal with it.

> Only in the detachment of an incurable complaint, in the sanity of near death, could one cope with this for a moment. In order to exist rationally, Pnin had taught himself, during the last ten years, never to remember Mira Belochkin—not because, in itself, the evocation of a youthful love affair, banal and brief, threatened his peace of mind (alas, recollections of his marriage to Liza were imperious enough to crowd out any former romance), but because, if one were quite sincere with oneself, no conscience, and hence no consciousness, could be expected to subsist in a world where such things as Mira's death were possible. (P,134–35)

Thus, Pnin's spatial and temporal exile involves something more than the loss of his country where home was defined; it involves the world of supposedly human beings who not only allow such things as Mira's death to occur but who also participate in them. It is not the truncated love *affair* that is painful to face, it is the destruction of the assumption that human beings are loving creatures. This is a more profound exile.

In his condition of exile Pnin goes about the charade of quotidian existence, but of the many activities with which he occupies himself only one seems to be of any real importance to him, his research. It is the one activity which one might venture to call "normal" that touches the possibility of a whole self, or, perhaps more accurately, fuses the disparate selves he is composed of in the way that memory and his seizures do.

Fittingly, his subject is a history of Russian culture, but a particular kind of history: "A *Petite Histoire* . . . in which a choice of Russian curiosities, Customs, and Literary Anecdotes, and so forth would be presented in such a way as to reflect in miniature *la Grande Histoire*—Major Concatenations of Events" (P, 76). His sense of his subject is itself a reflection of the way in which the novel is composed—a focus on the concatenation of small events, obliquely and peripherally presented—and it echoes as well, in the phrase "reflect in miniature," Victor's approach to his art, which has been associated with Van Eyck's tiny convex mirrors.

The relationship between what he reads and thinks about as he conducts his research in the carrel, and the scenes from the past he is able to keep alive through memory, is evident.[12] There are, however, more complicated connections Nabokov knits into the fabric. I have mentioned the association of water with exile in another context; that association is approached through Pnin's research, as well. As he reads the passage about

12. An instance of the complex reticulation Nabokov can create even when using apparently stale idiomatic phraseology is appropriate to cite here: "No gallery connected Waindell College Library with any other buildings, but it was intimately and securely connected with Pnin's heart" (P, 72).

the pagan rites of Green Week in Kostromskoy's volume on Russian myths, he is struck not simply by the description of peasant maidens making wreathes and singing and garlanding the willows, but also by a "curious verbal association" which he cannot specify. After looking up the correct pronunciation of "interested" in Webster, the association miraculously clarifies itself:

> . . . plila i pela, pela i plila . . .
> . . . she floated and she sang, she sang and floated . . .
> Of course! Ophelia's death! Hamlet! (P, 79)

He notes the similarities between the scenes of Ophelia's suicide and of the peasant maidens' activities, and thus explains to himself why the association occurred in his mind. But the pattern is wider than he is aware. When he was having trouble making the association conscious, the narrator dropped in a suggestive adjective: "He could not catch it by its *mermaid* tail" (P,77, my italics). The word is fitting, of course, since the maidens are floating among the loosed garlands, and Ophelia is herself in a like situation, weeded, though dead. But it is intended to lead the reader, if not Pnin, to recall Joan Clements' attempt after Liza's visit to cheer Pnin by means of a cartoon in a magazine: "'This is a desert island with a lone palm, and this is a bit of broken raft, and this is a shipwrecked mariner, and this is the ship's cat he saved . . . and this is a rather wistful mermaid hanging around'" (P, 60). Pnin is implicitly in such a situation himself, without the mermaid, and we are again in the presence of his islanded life, "floating and singing." His direct response to the cartoon is in terms of literature—he starts to comment on two poems by Lermontov —which may be said to lead us back to his library carrel; his response to the whole experience of which Joan's effort is the last stage is to say, sobbing, "I haf nofing left, nofing, nofing" (P, 61). The short association between the peasant girls and the scene from *Hamlet* is apparently superficial and transient for Pnin, but it serves a more complicated purpose for the novel, revealing again that nothing is disconnected from Pnin's bereft condition.

Pnin's sense of the burdensomeness of keeping "a particle of one's childhood in contact with one's breastbone," which I have commented on in another context, is similarly handled from the vantage of his research. In the only other passage in which he goes into any detail about his studies, the narrator says that "this research had long entered the charmed stage when the quest overrides the goal, and a new organism is formed, the parasite so to speak of the ripening fruit" (P, 143). Recall that, in the context of his first seizure, Pnin had been spoken of as regarding his heart "with a queasy dread, a nervous repulsion, a sick hate, as if it were some strong slimy untouchable monster that one had to be parasitized with, alas" (P, 20). Without freezing the connection into a mathematical equation one becomes aware of the paradoxical characteristics of Pnin's possible identity: the demands of integrity and sanity make him keep the past alive since it offers the only way (short of dying) out of exile, and yet this very effort becomes a profound burden, because it dramatizes emotionally the condition it seeks to alter; exile is unnatural, and causes one to employ unnatural methods of living with it. To attempt to live creatively within a situation that is intolerable means continuously to be aware of the situation itself. All one's ruses become reminders.

The *form* of the novel, as I have been suggesting, communicates this without letup. No matter where one enters it he is led to central foci; with respect to the particular entrance I am presently in the midst of, Pnin's research, there is another detail that affords similar connections perhaps more obviously than either the "mermaid" association or the quest of the heart as parasitic. I'm referring to the squirrel, who keeps popping up throughout the book.

In the first passage devoted to his studies Pnin is described as if he is observed by other people in the library: "Many good young people considered it a treat and an honor to see Pnin pull out a catalogue drawer from the comprehensive bosom of a card cabinet and take it, *like a big nut*, to a secluded corner and there make a quiet meal of it" (P, 76, my italics). By itself this would be little more than a simile suggesting the pleasure of mental digestion, but it doesn't occur by itself. It may be seen as an explicit center of many suggestions radiating through the novel.

The squirrel appears first in the context of Timofey's first seizure: it is pictured on the wooden screen of his room in St. Petersburg. In his fever he becomes worried to figure out what the "reddish object" it holds in its front paws could be, a "dreary riddle" that is modulated into the riddle posed by the wallpaper, the solution of which would, Timofey thinks, mean restoration. As he emerges back into Whitchurch from the seizure the first thing he sees is "a gray squirrel sitting on comfortable haunches on the ground before him . . . sampling a peach stone" (P, 24).

The squirrel's second appearance occurs after Liza's visit, near the close of Pnin's day not long before the incident of the cartoon. Pnin is as close to open despair as he comes in the novel. "He seemed to be quite unexpectedly . . . on the verge of a simple solution of the universe but was interrupted by an urgent request. A squirrel under a tree had seen Pnin on the path" (P, 58). She jumps up on the water fountain Pnin is walking by and in all but words requests a drink. Pnin obliges, pressing the foot pedal that controls the flow of water. And then, "the water father continued upon his way" (P, 58).

When the animal makes its third appearance, Pnin is on his

way to the library for an afternoon with his research. He watches a squirrel, escaping the rocks of "delinquents," dash across a path of sunlight and hide himself in a tree. It is Pnin's birthday—he is fifty-five—[13] and as he slips on the icy pavement and regains his balance he thinks, as he has had occasion to do already in the morning, of the lines from a poem in which Pushkin wonders about the precise moment and place of his death.

All three of these occurrences precede the image of Pnin munching the "big nut" of the index card, and each one focuses suggestions that prepare for the implications of that comparison. In the first one the squirrel appears in the context of Pnin's "illness," the mode through which both time and place are suspended for Pnin and the concomitant suspension of his identity dramatized. In the second the context is Liza's disappointing visit and departure, the concatenation of themes involving Pnin's loss of his wife, his erstwhile son, and his identification as "water father," exiled and isolate. In both these instances, moreover, the squirrel is associated with Pnin's awareness of the need to find some key to the riddle of his life and the universe. In the third instance, the associations include the personalness of his teaching, and his consideration, through the prism of Pushkin's poem, of his own death.

13. There are many places at which this footnote could appear; I have chosen to put it here for convenience. The chapter in which this event occurs (Chapter 3) is wholly controlled by the importance of the date: February 15 (Gregorian calendar, or "disguise," as the narrator calls it), 1953. The narrator makes a little game of hiding while revealing that it is Pnin's birthday ("O careless reader!" p. 75), calling attention to the fact, of course, as though it is important. And it is, for each segment of the chapter points, gently and poignantly, to aspects of Pnin's exile. In his class he quotes Pushkin's poem, the lines of which recur to him after he watches the squirrel climb the tree; he goes to the library and eats his big nut and discovers his mermaid association; he goes to the Stern's Russian evening and sees movies of his homeland and returns to the Clements' weeping; finally, he even loses his room because Isabel, her marriage broken, returns. Each occurrence shimmers with loss—of his childhood, his homeland, his wife, his language, his current residence—so that the word "birthday" becomes resonant in a way it rarely is.

The complexity of these accumulated associations is intended to be evoked, I think, when Pnin is observed with that index card. His research is directed toward his own condition, into the dimensions of his exile, his isolation, his loss, and his fragmentation, the major themes which his own *petite histoire* adumbrates.

I don't wish to belabor this since it seems, if only because of the frequent recurrence of the squirrel, to be the most noticeable aspect of the novel's pattern. Nevertheless, it might be noted that the associations built around this detail extend, finally, beyond Pnin. Victor mails him a postcard with a picture of a gray squirrel on it, and the color of the bowl he sends to Pnin is discussed (at the party, especially p. 158) in terms that return to the squirrel, terms that add the story of Cinderella and her magic slipper to the earlier suggestions the little animal focuses. [14] Victor, then, would seem to be involved in a situation similar to that of his "water father," himself exiled and deprived. From that perspective his art assumes an importance analogous to Pnin's research. There is, in fact, something uncannily prophetic about the whole coincidental series, for, chronologically in Pnin's life (though placed near the novel's end), the first appearance of the squirrel is on a shelf of his boyhood room (P, 177).

III   THE NARRATOR

Pnin is an imaginative construction of the terms by means of which exile can be confronted, an engagement of possibilities in a world where only possibilities can be engaged. This is also true of Pnin. The sources of identity are lost—that is the given in which the composition resides; yet there is also the given necessity that they not be lost irrevocably. The composition is thus formed to give the illusion of biography as

14. And through the addition swing us back to the terms of Lake's color theory.

though that illusion is a mirror image of a basic need, an identity that can be believed, and believed in.

The illusion, then, is purposeful, as all illusions are. It is, primarily, the narrator's illusion, and the basic need it mirrors is his own. He must create a "Pnin" who can be believed in as an object of biography, a person who can be *spoken of as if* he has an independent existence. Why? Because "Pnin" is a name for a particular identity which is not only *formed by* a condition of exile, but *is* a condition of exile as well. As such it is possible identity *for the narrator*, who is an émigré exile himself. "Pnin" must be confronted, known, ejected and replaced so the narrator may be free of the possibility he embodies.

As a textbook might phrase it, the narrator consciously objectifies a possible alternative in Pnin in order to exorcise it. Pnin is a fabrication but he is real; he is lovable, poignant, dedicated, and because of these qualities he is dangerous, since they make the condition of exile he presents attractive. For he is, with all his bumbling generosity and unselfishness, basically a victim of his losses, meshed in patterns of endless recurrence, and the moral value of the experience of the novel lies in the narrator's choice of refusing to play that role himself.

In this light, the narrator's replacement of Pnin at Waindell becomes a fulfillment, metaphorically, of the threat he poses to Pnin from the novel's beginning. As Pnin's creator he may also be Pnin's disposer. Hence Pnin's hostility toward him; hence the narrator's ability to afford the attitudes of tenderness and amusement toward Pnin, although I think these latter attitudes are more than a function of condescension: the narrator is, after all, deciding against alternatives he finds available to himself, and he is sympathetic toward them. If he weren't, there would be no need for the novel.

To return to the considerations I suggested at the close of part I of this chapter, I hope I have shown that Pnin is a convenience of immense importance. He must seem as true a biographical figure as possible because *he is a life*, a life the narrator envisions and, eventually, supplants. But, simultaneously, he is an imaginative invention, and the reader must be as continually aware of that as he is of the biographical design. In the phrase "biographical illusion" both terms are indispensable.

The illusion gets the accent, however, because the context is finally, and always, a book. The narrator's need cannot be fulfilled except through the creation of Pnin, which is to say through composition. Perhaps this is analogous to the author's relationship to *Pnin*. Who knows?[15] At any rate, the novel realizes a simultaneous defeat and victory, out of which perhaps emerges a dignity and hope, but not in such highfalutin terms as these. Pnin passes that beer truck, and perhaps shares somehow in the victory (as the narrator shares in defeat), for "there was simply no saying what miracle might happen." For, as the narrator has exorcised Pnin, so Pnin is free of the narrator.

15. It *is* interesting, though, that the émigré Russians at Al Cook's discuss, among other writers, Sirin (P,117), and at least one of them (Chateau) regrets the absence of "Vladimir Vladimirovich" and assures Pnin of the genuineness of V.V.'s entomology (P,128). Finally, from the perspective my reading affords, the famous lecturer whose visit to Waindell impends, merges with Nabokov only after passing through the image of the narrator; in this particular, as in more general considerations in this and other chapters (especially Chapter Five), my emphasis and implication veer away from Andrew Field's in his informative book, *Nabokov: His Life in Art* (Boston: Little, Brown and Company, 1967).

SEVEN

Speak, Memory: Autobiography as Fiction

I would not appear to approach *Speak, Memory* as though to exhaust it, as perhaps in these previous chapters I have appeared to do with some of Vladimir Nabokov's other books. I would rather seem to dance around it, as I believe it does around itself, so to speak, to echo its overtones, or some such figuratively acrobatic critical maneuver. The trouble is, one of the functions of these essays is to elucidate—to find what the sailor has hidden and point toward it—and as such they work at cross-purposes with the books they focus on. The author's pleasure in assembling the disguised bird who seems part of the twig on which it rests is different from the reader's pleasure in discovering it, and removed still farther from the critical pleasure of reassembly. In this primary respect literary criticism is always performed among the echoes of Jack Horner's plangent cry.

I am tempted to say that *Speak, Memory* is the book on which Nabokov spent his most painstaking care, but that isn't so; there are no degrees of attention in his work, and each has been nurtured as thoroughly as possible. But *Speak, Memory* is the book he has most frequently written, or rewritten, or, as he characterized his last venture into its composition, revisited. No less than all his other books, it is a construction, in his words "A *systematically correlated* assemblage of personal recollections."[1] It is an autobiography, but it is not a record, or account, of facts (that troublesome curbing one keeps stumbling over). It is imaginative narration in which events, actions, details of landscape (both indoors and out) in themselves neutral, are formed, shaped, and rendered significant by a single, ordering consciousness. It is, in short, fiction, a molding (*fingere*), not opposed to fact—the popular distinction one is numbed into accepting as a habit of daily perception—but the way fact is born. The opposite of fiction is Nothing, the famous Void, *rien*, *nada*, the Big Blank. The rawest material is the alphabet, containing the building blocks we put together one way and another to invent ourselves and the worlds we people.[2] One could debate the assertion that all autobiography

1. *Speak, Memory: An Autobiography Revisited* (Rev. ed.; New York: G. P. Putnam and Sons, 1966), 9, my italics. All subsequent quotations are from this edition and are followed by page numbers in parentheses. The brief theoretical remarks that follow on the fiction of autobiography are both personal inclination and intellectual choice. Nonetheless, some of Nabokov's remarks about related matters bear on my position. Those most pertinent appear in interviews collected and reprinted in *Strong Opinions*: see the comments on pages 12 ("Memory is . . . a tool . . ."), 142 ("Yes—unless I refashion . . ."), 154 ("The simultaneousness of these random events . . .") and the entries "Personal Past," "Ancestral Past," and "Family Tree" on pages 186–87.

2. Fiction is not opposed to Truth, either—another lumpish tradition. Rather, we judge truth and falsehood from the perspective of fiction, some construction or other to which we commit ourselves. This perspective can be more devastatingly disconcerting when a life is predicated on it, as one is in Nabokov's last novel, *Look at the Harlequins* (New York: McGraw-Hill, 1974). Compared to the curlicues and sidles Vadim McNab, the narrator of that book, has to deal with, the conception which this chapter of mine confronts is a piece of cake.

In addition to the puzzling (to him) burden of his truncated names, McNab has to manage not just the fact that he is Nabokov's only *bellelettrist* narrator, but as well the echoes which resound between the titles of his novels and those of his creator (of whom he is at times dimly aware). Some are loud indeed: the narrator's *Camera Lucida* and Nabokov's *Kamera Obskura*, or *Dr. Olga Repnin* and *Pnin*, or *Ardis* and *Ada*. Others are less audible: McNab's *Plenilune* is a novel in verse in Russian; Nabokov's *Pale Fire* is not entirely in verse, and was composed in English; the naris fiction (a complimentary, not a pejorative, assertion); in the case of *Speak, Memory*, however, Nabokov encourages the perspective I have chosen to emphasize. To assemble and correlate systematically is to make fiction, neither a surprising nor a profound critical observation, but as far as I know to have that mode of arrangement inform an autobiography is unusual at least, and to find it done as well as Nabokov does it is remarkable.

I

In Chapter 1 ("Perfect Past"), Section 3, General Kuropatkin, while visiting the Nabokovs (in 1904), is informed

----

rator's *Pawn Takes Queen* seems a composite of Nabokov's *King, Queen, Knave* and *The Defense*; and *See Under Real* (McNab) seems to combine compositional elements of both *The Real Life of Sebastian Knight* and *Pale Fire*.

That data suggests and denies simultaneously any identification between the two memoirists, Nabokov and McNab. For, indeed, as McNab sees it, *Look at the Harlequins* is his memoirs, an "oblique autobiography—oblique, because dealing mainly not with pedestrian history but with the mirages of romantic and literary matters," a "story of love and prose."

The memoir, of course, mimics *Speak, Memory*, and at the appropriate places the style and voice of McNab's account echo those of the various novels from which his own derive.

For McNab *is* a derivation, a parody, of his maker. And yet, as he is not a copy Nabokov so neither he nor the book he writes is strictly self-parody. It is rather self-parody as metaphor, an entertainment of a possibility. It is as if one seeks to discover how fiction can be employed to create its author, a step beyond the relatively simple consideration of one's autobiography as fiction. In the context of his own "reconstruction" McNab says, "It had never occurred to me before that, historically, art, or at least artifacts, had preceded, not followed, nature; yet that is exactly what happened in my case" (LH, 244).

The experience of *Look at the Harlequins* broadly expressed is the continuous test of what identity can be derived from the fictions attributed to it. This testing is then shifted to an oblique angle when the tester (Nabokov) makes the fictions parodies of other fictions: his own books become models on which are based the novels from which the identity of an author (fictional himself, a third harlequin) can emerge.

We do not know either Nabokov's novels, or Nabokov, by reading *Look at the Harlequins*, but we do encounter a tentative and tenuous identity seeking its periled and perilous self through its work. The novel dramatizes what it would be like if one were to draw himself out of his fictions, not simply make his life fictional. Thus to commit parody is to open a set of Chinese boxes. When one recognizes the terrific infinity of this he must realize both his power and responsibility, which is to say walk with skill and grace the thin edge between frivolity and comedy.

165

that he has been made commander of the Russian army in the Far East. The particular activity that this announcement interrupts is the general's performing for young Vladimir a simple "trick" with matchsticks. Fifteen years later, Vladimir's father, fleeing St. Petersburg, gives a light to a stranger on a bridge in southern Russia. In the glare of the match the stranger turns out to be Kuropatkin, disguised, himself in flight. Nabokov comments: "What pleases me is the evolution of the match theme: those magic ones he had shown me had been trifled with and mislaid, and his armies had also vanished." He concludes the section by declaring, "The following of such thematic designs through one's life should be, I think, the true purpose of autobiography."

Very straightforward and explicit: the general rule, the specific instance illustrating it. Another instance, however, is being carried on at the same time, without comment. Just prior to presenting Kuropatkin, Nabokov has shown us some war pictures (1904) by Japanese artists "that showed how the Russian locomotives—made singularly toylike by the Japanese pictorial style—would drown if our Army tried to lay rails across the treacherous ice of Lake Baikal." Kuropatkin intervenes with his matches, then in disguise, as if to replace the toylike trains, but their image is simply deferred. The sentence in which the "match theme" is explicitly mentioned goes on: ". . . and everything had fallen through, like my toy trains that, in the winter of 1904–05, in Wiesbaden, I tried to run over the frozen puddles in the grounds of the Hotel Oranien."

This is, I think, a rather noticeable instance of Nabokov's doing more than he calls one's attention to; its purpose here is at least to alert his reader to the nature of the book as a whole: not only will he "follow thematic designs," he will also *not* point them all out. Moreover, the one he *doesn't* point out here is the more poignant of the two, is complementary to the first and therefore deepens its emotional effect, and, finally, reveals what is basic to the design of both: the theme of exile, of it "all falling through," one of the basic perspectives from which the autobiography is constructed.

It shouldn't be surprising that another such perspective is art itself, surfacing naturally as a theme in the life of a writer, but present everywhere as the indispensable mode through which all other themes and objects are rendered. The subject of Chapter 2, for instance, is Nabokov's mother. Among other subtleties (to which I will return in a later context) he makes the theme of verbal composition pulse constantly through the chapter's first two sections, without speaking explicitly of it until he has nearly finished. He accomplishes this through the alphabet blocks which he mentions while discussing his *audition coloree,* and through the gigantic Faber pencil his mother brings him while he is ill. When he receives the pencil he checks to make sure the point is real graphite (it is), "and some years later I satisfied myself, by drilling a hole in the side, that the lead went right through the whole length—a perfect case of art for art's sake" (SM, 39). Up until that explicit acknowledgment, however, he has presented both experiences so that the *form* of their presentation mirrors the form of recollection: that is, the blocks and the pencil are singled out because they are significant, bearing the suggestion of the beginnings of a line of experience that will be central to the autobiographer's life, yet the child who played with the blocks and received the pencil was not aware of any such significance at the time. Both the adult's consciousness at the time of writing and the child's consciousness at the time of playing coexist in the assembly of the recollection. Because of Nabokov's skill one experiences this dramatically, rather than being told about it.

Chapter 4 focuses its attention on the various aspects of Anglo-Saxon culture that influenced aristocratic Russian families at the turn of the century, and therefore helped compose what Nabokov calls "my English education." There were soaps and tub baths and halberdiers and a series of nurses, governesses, and tutors—a wealth of detail, all of which, however eclectically it may seem to be gathered, is being aimed carefully. Here are two targets.

About halfway through Chapter 4, young Vladimir's progress bedward at the end of a day comes to a conclusion simultaneously with the section (3) which presents it. Among the objects in his room is "a framed aquarelle" which "showed a dusky path winding through one of those eerily dense European beechwoods, where the only undergrowth is hindweed and the only sound one's thumping heart." He recalls a small boy in an English fairy tale who stepped out of his bed into a picture, and imagines for himself "the motion of climbing into the picture above my bed and plunging into that enchanted beechwood—which I did visit in due time." *Due time* in this case means roughly eight pages, for the chapter ends with Nabokov and M. V. Dobuzhinski, in the nineteen-forties, strolling "through a beech forest in Vermont." In this instance pictorial art provides the context for the fillip to the theme of imaginative composition.

That short conversation with Dobuzhinski in Vermont, which occupies but two brief paragraphs, affords the other target, too, a further complexity, rounding the chapter back into itself with a tactic similar to the one used earlier with the matches and trains. The setup, concerned with three drawing teachers, is carefully done. From the first, Dobuzhinski, who taught him to "depict from memory, in the greatest possible detail, objects I had certainly seen thousands of times without visualizing them properly," Nabokov concludes that he gained ability that, though it didn't reveal itself in his youth, stood him in good stead later in his drawings of butterfly genitalia and in "certain camera-lucida needs of literary composition." About the other two, a Scotsman named Burness and Mr. Cummings, an illustrator from London, he learns things as an adult that as their pupil he never suspected, and in the learning he experiences "a queer shock; it was as if life had impinged upon my creative rights by wriggling on beyond the subjective limits so elegantly and economically set by childhood memories that I thought I had signed and sealed."

What happens then, in the economical chat with Dobuzhinski that immediately follows, is that the *other* "signed and sealed" conclusion about profiting from Dobuzhinski's teaching is shown to have *its* subjective limits, too. "I do know," says the old teacher, "that *you* were the most hopeless pupil I ever had." What appears, then, to be a haphazard, in fact strange, structural addition—the last two paragraphs of the chapter, tacked on, it seems at first, for no earthly reason—is in fact the stroke that makes the chapter whole and purposeful instead of random, and reminds us by making us experience it that what we are reading has been composed, and is neither accidental nor an amanuensis slavish listing of "what happened."[3]

I have selected these representative, or illustrative, instances from the earlier chapters of *Speak, Memory* because I think Nabokov has had to be more circumspect in their construction than in the making of the last third of the book (Chapters 11 through 18). He has had to make the themes of exile and art present and effectual in these chapters but, as I have suggested, remain "true" to the perspective of his character (himself as a child) as well. This is not to say, however, that when he begins to speak of these two themes directly and extensively that he abandons subtlety and circuitousness. Section 2 of Chapter

3. The two-paragraph exchange between Nabokov and Dobuzhinski, which itself violates the apparent "signed and sealed" feeling of Chapter 4, is, like much of what I think makes *Speak, Memory* a magnificent book, not included in the earlier versions, whether titled *Conclusive Evidence* or *Speak, Memory*. Only the edition I am using contains it. Someone more temperamentally inclined than I am to such activity will surely write about the various stages Nabokov's autobiography has gone through. It is not, however, my purpose here.

14, for example, begins with the implicit equation of his early novels and the autobiography his reader is engaged with. "I have sufficiently spoken of the gloom and the glory of exile in my Russian novels, and especially in the best of them, *Dar* . . . but a quick recapitulation here may be convenient" (SM, 280). The striking word is "sufficiently"; the striking effect is the ease with which the author veers away from his initial focus, the end of the sentence being at a significant remove from its beginning. The job is done, however, and though he may ignore it the reader has been "told" that not only are novel and autobiography brothers under the label but also, in this case anyway, the former is sufficient and the latter adjunctive.

That reversal of a traditional habit of literary perception is followed not long after by, as it were, a short turn on the trapeze. He concludes his "recapitulation" with a brief commentary on the émigré writers of his two decades in Europe, among whom he lists Sirin, "the author that interested me most." Sirin is, of course, the pen name Nabokov used during the period,[4] and he thus comments on his own work in the third person, as if it had been done by someone else. And I suppose in a way it had been, the Nabokov writing the autobiography including but not limited to the man he was thirty years previously. The use of the pseudonym is suggestive, too, a nice emblem for the act of making one's self up, in which process the autobiographer is engaged. It is also a rather blatant instance of trickery on his part, but by this point in the book one should be ready for that; if not, he learns, because within three pages one's elusive guide has confronted him with the particular pleasures of the composition of chess problems and

---

4. My second, and final, comparison of the 1966 edition of *Speak, Memory* to its earlier varieties is motivated by a desire for symmetry. In this instance the game of the "final" version is more devious and fascinating because of deletions: in *Conclusive Evidence* Nabokov mentioned both *Invitation to a Beheading* and *Luzhin's Defense* as works by Sirin. No longer is that assignment made, however, so the identification of the man behind the allusion is more difficult.

their association with the pleasures of literary composition, stressing "originality" and "deceit to the point of diabolism."

To the themes, or, as I have been calling them, perspectives, of exile and art, I would add a third, the grand theme, one might say, of all autobiography, time. As with the previous focuses, what I wish to call attention to is how Nabokov leads one to experience his manipulation of time, the instances of time as drama, rather than the commentary on time as an idea which surfaces occasionally. One clear and explicit purpose of *Speak, Memory* is, of course, to make immortal what might otherwise be totally lost, obliterated by the Paduks and paddocks of history. To set it down, however, is worse than insufficient: the chronologic of a record intensifies the tyranny of time. To overthrow it one must reconstruct according to other principles of order.

Rudimentary, which is to say undisguised, signals of this perspective are dispersed throughout the book. In Chapter 2 Vladimir's mother bursts into tears when her sons, having violated her wishes by going through the contents of their Christmas stockings the night before, fail on the critical morning to reenact convincingly their earlier surprise and pleasure. In the next sentence "A decade passed." In the next "World War One started." In the same paragraph Mrs. Nabokov sets up a private hospital for wounded soldiers, and her son remembers her "denouncing with *the same childish tears* the impenetrable meekness of those crippled peasants and the ineffectiveness of part-time compassion" (my italics). Perspective, the commitment to a particular fiction, determines value: the eye of the author, as opposed, say, to the eye of an "objective historian," sees those tears in radically different relation to such "events" as a world war, or the passing of ten years.

A similar obviousness pertains in the first section of "Mademoiselle O." Almost *ab nihil* (his memory provides only a scrap or two to work with) Nabokov creates the arrival of his new French governess (winter 1905/1906) at the Siverski railroad station six miles by sleigh from the Nabokov country estate. He has her mount the sleigh; the speed rises, the moon rises, she is cold, the snow bears the tracks of the runners, "every sparkling lump of snow is emphasized by a swollen shadow." And then this coda:

> Very lovely, very lonesome. But what am I doing in this stereo-scopic dreamland? How did I get here? Somehow, the two sleighs have slipped away, leaving behind a passportless spy standing on the blue-white road in his New England snowboots and stormcoat. All is still, spellbound, enthralled by the moon, fancy's rear-vision mirror. The snow is real, though, and as I bend to it and scoop up a handful, sixty years crumble to glittering frost-dust between my fingers. (SM,99–100)

This is similar to stepping into the painting of the beech forest and across thirty years to chat with a former instructor, and in fact follows it, in the next section of the book.

If such patterns do not adequately signify the compositional nature of time as it is being structurally defined, then other instances are terminologically more direct. Great-grandfather Nikolay discovered a river in Nova Zembla;[5] great-grandson Vladimir described a new butterfly in Colorado: thus "Nabokov's River (1817) figures "Nabokov's Pug" (1943), or vice versa. Kin to that is another ancestral echo: a paternal forebear, Baroness Von Korff, in 1791 in Paris lent passport and carriage to the royal family "for their escape to Varennes"; Nabokov's father, in 1917, is unable to grant a similar aid to Kerenski because he has no suitable vehicle. Nabokov "treasures the recollection," he says, "only from a compositional viewpoint," and leaves it to the reader to notice the numerical anagram of the dates. Another explicit acknowledgment of the "compositional viewpoint" that shows how *much* time Nabo-

---

5. Nabokov's parenthetical comment is "of all places."

kov is manipulating (time is a measure: if you can pour a quart of water from one container to another, why not an hour of time?) is the piecing together of shards of majolica less than two pages from the end of the book. The viewpoint, as *my* structure implies, is more deviously patterned, however, on other occasions. Notice for example the following transition between paragraphs: Vladimir is reading a poem to his mother, in Berlin on the night of March 28, 1922; responding to an image in it she says, over her knitting,

> "Yes, yes, Florence does look like a *dïmnïy iris*, how true! I remember—" when the telephone rang.
> After 1923, when she moved to Prague.... (SM,49)

A hiatus, yes; incoherence, no. The time that has been omitted will not be poured into the gap all at once, either; nor will it be accompanied by any more fanfare than it is here. In the next chapter, densely populated by ancestors, the stage is occupied a while by Dmitri Nabokov, Vladimir's paternal grandfather. He devotes a good deal of attention to the rather elaborate illusion (making the old man's bedroom in St. Petersburg look like the one he had in Nice) practiced by his (V.N.'s) mother during Dmitri's last days. The artistry succeeds: when the grandfather is awake he believes he is on the Riviera, "and there," writes the grandson, "on March 28, 1904, exactly eighteen years day for day, before my father, he peacefully died" (SM,59). Ten pages later and, as it were, eighteen years earlier, the reason for the telephone's rude interruption, and for the third-person singular, feminine pronoun in the opening sentence of the following paragraph, is revealed, though the magician is pointing somewhere else.

Such misdirection, though Nabokov makes a stunningly inverted use of it, characterizes the chapter which most delicately and beautifully incarnates the kind of control and drama I have been discussing. It is fitting that butterflies, because of their instaric lives, and their almost timeless association with the soul, are the focus of the chapter.[6] Although there is much discussion of various catches and caches, the real subject is only one chase and one discovery, the literary re-creation of which acts as the embodiment of the ecstasy Nabokov finds in butterfly hunting.

This central experience is alluded to immediately, twice, in fact, in the brief opening section.

> The foliage of birches [at Vyra] moving in the sun had the translucent green tone of grapes, and in contrast to this there was the dark velvet of fir trees against a blue of extraordinary intensity, the like of which I rediscovered only many years later, in the montane zone of Colorado. (SM, 119)

And

> On the following morning, however, when she unlocked the wardrobe to take something out, my Swallowtail, with a mighty rustle, flew into her face, then made for the open window, and presently was but a golden fleck dripping and dodging and soaring eastward, over timber and tundra, to Vologda, Viatka and Perm, and beyond the gaunt Ural range to Yakutsk and Verkhne Kolymsk, and from Verkhne Kolymsk, where it lost a tail, to the fair Island of St. Lawrence, and across Alaska to Dawson, and southward along the Rocky Mountains—to be finally overtaken and captured, after a forty-year race, on an immigrant dandelion under an endemic aspen near Boulder. (SM, 120)

Both passages *seem* direct, but they are at least coy. In the first there is nothing (but the meagerly developed context—and even that isn't announced yet, since the chapters do not bear in the book the titles they did in serial publication) to indicate it refers to hunting butterflies, which we later learn Nabokov was doing in Colorado. And in the second the Swallowtail itself commands the dips and glides of the sentence; by the time

---

6. Six, called "Butterflies." Section 2 of the chapter concludes with the much-noted paragraph about the "nonutilitarian delights" of nature and art.

it is captured (we learn, by the by, the city in Colorado near which the netting occurred) the agent of its capture is at best in the wings.

A third reference appears six pages later. This time Nabokov, through the dates 1910 and 1943, delimits the "forty-year race" more precisely,[7] associates the pursuit with literary activity through the mention of his first American publisher,[8] and extends "the thematic spiral" back to his great-grandfather's discovery in 1817. At this point one expects the chase and capture, some of whose shadows and highlights have been allusively sketched, to recur, perhaps climactically, in detail subsequently in the chapter. It is certainly being "announced" in Nabokov's most arch and self-delighting manner.

Well, it does recur, of course, and it is climactic, but it is unannounced after all, except in the terms used already to prepare for it. "There came a July day—around 1910, I suppose—" Nabokov writes, and the chase begins with his "urge to explore the vast marshland beyond the Ordezh." He does, in minute detail, and a vast marsh it is, for by the time he comes to its end he finds on the rising ground beyond "a paradise of lupines, columbines, and pentstemons. Mariposa lilies bloomed under Ponderosa pines. In the distance, fleeting cloud shadows dappled the dull green of slopes above timber line, and the gray and white of Longs Peak" (SM, 139). We are in Colorado. And having been wafted there surreptitiously, having had, indeed, to compose quite literally our journey there, Nabokov, still not done with his game of What Shade Scumbles the Nymphet, says, "I confess I do not believe in time. I like to fold my magic carpet, after use, in such a way as to superimpose one part of the pattern upon another. Let visitors trip." Nabokov "confesses" unnecessarily because he

7. The chase I discuss as "one" may well be a composite.
8. The echo of another pursuit haunts the entire chapter, not least through the evocation of "Dolly. Dolores, Colorado."

has enacted the belief already. But he has also challenged the reader, and the gauntlet of those three sentences makes it official.

II

In "that strange first decade of our century" the peasants from the village near Vyra would occasionally request a favor from Vladimir Dmitrievich Nabokov. "If, as usually happened, the request was at once granted... in token of gratitude, the good *barin* would be put through the national ordeal of being rocked and tossed up and securely caught by a score or so of strong arms." Young Vladimir Vladimirovich, from his seat at the dining table, could see only the airborne part of the ceremony. "For an instant, the figure of my father in his wind-rippled white summer suit would be displayed, gloriously sprawling in mid-air, his limbs in a curiously casual attitude, his handsome, imperturbable features turned to the sky" (SM, 31). Thrice the father soars, each time higher, until "on his last and loftiest flight," he reclines "as if for good, against the cobalt blue of the summer noon."

This (which I have not reproduced completely) is one of the most marvelous, arresting, and moving scenes in all of Nabokov. It carries with natural grace immeasurable weight: from the child's seat in the dining room what is seen (and overheard) suggests the stability and strength of the father's world (and therefore the child's); the revolutionary rumblings, the Tsarist oppression, are at a distance and the father keeps them there. At home he is the *barin*, yet he has spent time in solitary confinement for opposition to the government that has dissolved his parliament. The relationship between village peasant and aristocratic landowner is shown to be different from what most history texts broadcast, yet, quite literally, the father's life is in the hands of peasants. The suspension of the

father "as if for good," *a la* cherubim in a cathedral, introduces a central thrust of the book's energy, yet this is counter-
poised by the ambiguous coffin. Is it empty or not? One cannot tell whom, if anyone, it contains. The only comment
comes from the oldest person present, Madame Nabokov's
governess, who says, resonantly, "Un jour ils vont le laisser
tomber."

In the first sentence of the section (5, of Chapter 1) Nabokov
suggests various themes which "got fantastically interwoven"
during those years, and by implication will be interwoven in
the scene he is about to describe, but as usual in the rare world
where imagination touches—deftly, lovingly—its sources,
here the tableau alone is far more complexly suggestive than
any accompanying gloss, including this one.

III

The immortality conferred on one's past by the composition of an autobiography is obviously a limited one, depending
as it does on habits that are themselves mortal: manufacture
—of paper, ink, type, and, with such tools, books; occupa-
tion—editing, publishing, bookselling, and most important,
of course, reading. Such activities are by no means guaranteed.
The future of the word, especially the printed word, is pre-
carious at best, and the thought that in some distant century
a few men will dig up an old, decomposing book and reinvent
the arts of reading and writing is of no solace whatever to those
who watch their decline.

Yet, before the *first* invention of printing, men were effective in making themselves immortal through recreative preser-
vation, and without books and readers will probably be so in
the future, as many illiterate people are now. There is a more
basic difficulty: whether the *means* of autobiographical immortality are printed or oral, the *terms* are mortal, inescapa-

bly, fittingly. The stuff of memory, and memory itself, is trapped in time; to compose an autobiography is to define a mortal and temporal confinement.

In the case of *Speak, Memory*, however, the composition is also a gentle but passionate bridling against that confinement. I have quoted Nabokov's "confession" that he didn't believe in time (though he lived and wrote in it); that belief (I switch to the positive, never defined) helps inform more than his composition of the pursuit of *Eupithecia nabokovi* (though that pursuit, and its object, are emblematic). Nabokov begins the book with this focus, and *belief* immediately becomes a term closer to Paul's "conviction of things not seen" than to the popular sense of "have the opinion that." Instead of a substitute for thought (as in "I believe" or "I feel") it is a mode of perception of a different order altogether. "Over and over again," he writes, "my mind has made colossal efforts to distinguish the faintest of personal glimmers in the impersonal darkness on both sides of my life. That this darkness is caused merely by the walls of time separating me and my bruised fists from the free world of timelessness is a belief I gladly share with the most gaudily painted savage" (SM, 20). Time becomes, as one becomes conscious, a prison to escape from. This kind of perception is religious, though not institutional or a matter of formal dogma; Nabokov cites intimate precedence for it when he says of his mother, "Her intense and pure religiousness took the form of her having equal faith in the existence of another world and in the impossibility of comprehending it in terms of earthly life" (SM, 39). Mortal terms will do for an autobiography, and for the suggestion of something beyond its fictional boundaries, but whatever *is* out there cannot be rendered.

In *Speak, Memory*, therefore, it isn't, but hints and hunches abound. They may be as tenuous as the looper caterpillar "measuring, like a child's finger and thumb, the rim of the table, and every now and then stretching upward to grope, in vain, for the shrub from which it had been dislodged" (SM,44), or as the Golliwog book about two airships, one huge, and one tiny for "the sole use of the fortunate Midget. At the immense altitude to which the ship reached, the aeronauts huddled together for warmth while the lost little soloist, still the object of my intense envy notwithstanding his plight, drifted into an abyss of frost and stars—alone" (SM,83). They may be more explicitly suggestive, as young Vladimir's ritual bedtime ascent with his eyes closed. "True," he writes, "the whole going-up-the-stairs business now reveals certain transcendental values" (SM,84). Yes, and those values are echoed without comment in a later passage in which the thematic design of the stairs is developed. Nabokov recalls the "snow-muffled house . . . built by my mother's grandfather, who, being afraid of fires, had the staircase fashioned of iron, so that when the house did get burned to the ground, sometime after the Soviet Revolution, those fine-wrought steps, with the sky shining through their openwork risers, remained standing, all alone but still leading up" (SM,100). And finally, they may be quite broadly direct, as in the last paragraph of Chapter 2. Nabokov says it is not in dreams, when one is aware of the dead without astonishment, when they appear tainted, "certainly not then . . . but when one is wide awake at moments of robust joy and achievement, on the highest terrace of consciousness, that mortality has a chance to peer beyond its own limits, from the mast, from the past and its castle tower. And though nothing much can be seen through the mist, there is somehow the blissful feeling that one is looking in the right direction" (SM,50). Thus consciousness, the dawning of which—racially and individually—Nabokov has said "must surely have coincided with the dawning of the sense of time" (SM, 21), also makes the plateau from which a man can look toward the eternity at the long end of his days. The source of the problem of temporal entrapment also provides the best means toward its dissolution.

For Nabokov, there are four accesses to that "highest terrace," or four names for being there: butterfly hunting, making poems, the composition of chess problems, and loving, which are interpenetrative and spoken of in terms of each other.[9] As "nothing much can be seen," so articulation of what is misted over on that terrace is, when Nabokov attempts it, comparative, spare.[10] His chapter on butterflies ends with these sentences:

> The highest enjoyment of timelessness... is when I stand among rare butterflies and their food plants. This is ecstasy, and behind the ecstasy is something else, which is hard to explain. It is like a momentary vacuum into which rushes all that I love. A sense of oneness with sun and stone. A thrill of gratitude to whom it may concern—to the contrapuntal genius of human fate or to tender ghosts humoring a lucky mortal. (SM, 139)

Most writers would be content with ecstasy, which is rare enough, but Nabokov suggests something else that ecstasy curtains. It is poignant, too, given the aim of the paragraph, that the object of gratitude is anthropomorphically conceived; that curtain is opaque, it seems, and whatever agency is responsible one can imagine it best in terms of one's own strengths: the fictional world that Nabokov composes in *Speak, Memory* (and elsewhere) is contrapuntal, and he is responsible for the tenderness with which *his* ghosts humor him.

About the composition of chess problems he says, echoing both terms and focus from the passage I have just quoted, "I do not seem to convey sufficiently the ecstatic core of the process and its points of connection with various other, more overt and

---

9. In *Strong Opinions* (40) Nabokov distinguishes between writing and butterfly hunting as different types of enjoyment.

10. See the stunning final remarks in the *Playboy* interview of 1964, in *Strong Opinions* (45).

fruitful, operations of the creative mind, from the charting of dangerous seas to the writing of one of those incredible novels where the author, in a fit of lucid madness, has set himself certain unique rules that he observes, certain nightmare obstacles that he surmounts, with the zest of a deity building a live world from the most unlikely ingredients—rocks, and carbon, and blind throbbings" (SM, 290). Typically, when the subject is intimate and a matter of passion, Nabokov distances it, speaking here, transparently I think, of himself as "the author." The comparison to a divine creator is explicit, if impersonal, and echoes, though it does not reproduce, the earlier "oneness with sun and stone."

That oneness and that divinity become the focus of Nabokov's crucial remarks about making poems and loving, in which passages space and time become sounds for synonymous phenomena, the former being a metaphor for the latter. I won't quote the relevant passages in their entirety because they are too long; the thrust of each is that the poet and the lover (a term not to be restricted to its erotic facet) is a center, a point, both temporal and spatial, to which an infinite variety of places and moments are connected, and in which they converge. "Tentacles," Nabokov says, "not wings, are Apollo's natural members" (SM, 218), and, in the context of thinking of his love for a person, "I am in the habit of immediately drawing radii from my love—from my heart, from the tender nucleus of a personal matter—to monstrously remote points of the universe" (SM, 296). In the latter case explicitly, and associatively in connection with the other three activities that compose the highest terrace of consciousness, he says, "I have to have all space and all time participate in my emotion, in my mortal love, so that the edge of its mortality is taken off, thus helping me to fight the utter degradation, ridicule, and horror of having developed an infinity of sensation and thought within a finite existence" (SM, 297). That angle gives a romantic glaze to Nabokov's notions, but he is not complaining, as Byron (or Hamlet) was; he is rather establishing a border so that he may suggest a dimension, and he does this with confidence, verve, and joy. Few men delight so consciously in the things of this world (to echo an old stance) while making unabashed suggestions that behind, or at the center of, the most ecstatic moments experience in this world offers there is *still* something else of another order altogether.[11]

IV

Chapter 2, which contains both the displaced looper caterpillar and the disruptive telephone, and concludes with Nabokov's remarks about the highest terrace of consciousness, is called "Portrait of my Mother." But long before it winds its way to lonely Prague and the concealing mist off yonder, it begins in another radiant place, just before the son's sleep, among his aural and optical visions. Nabokov presents these playfully, polysyllabically, and moves on to the phenomenon of his colored hearing. "Perhaps 'hearing' is not quite accurate," he explains, "since the color sensation seems to be produced by the very act of my orally forming a given letter while I imagine its outline" (SM, 34). There follows a precise detailing of the colors each letter evokes, and even a citation of the first author to discuss *audition coloree*.

An odd way to begin a portrait of his mother, one might say, until this distinction, disguised by the tone of factual reportage and authorial apology, occurs: "The confessions of a synesthete must sound tedious and pretentious to those who are protected from such leakings and drafts by more solid walls than mine are. To my mother though, this all seemed quite nor-

11. See my earlier comments on the spiral in the chapter on *Pnin*, and the opening paragraph of Chapter 14 of *Speak, Memory*. Certain of Nabokov's poems are suggestive in this context, too, notably "I Still Keep Mute" and "I Like that Mountain" (*Poems and Problems*, New York: McGraw-Hill, 1970), 25, 35.

mal" (SM, 35). He approaches his "subject" as if she were not a subject at all, but someone with whom he has a relationship that is so basic as to be a context that precedes any other subject. The *relationship* is the subject, then, the approach to the other person; Nabokov, in the lovely, oblique, sidling form of the chapter, embodies a truth something like this: a child knows a parent not so much as an objective, separate person, but as someone in concert with himself. The development of consciousness and age gradually effects the sense of separateness and distance, the emergence of mother into person. Yet the separation is not a severance, as the eminence of the chapter's end suggests.

V

Let's trace some images, follow a few thematic designs. A number of patterns are brief and tantalizing, windows through which one might glimpse a casual gesture opening into a profound secret, if they weren't so misty and if one was allowed to look long enough. The cigarette case for example, which so long resisted being clearly remembered: when Ordo, the spelling master in the summer of 1907, drops it, young Vladimir helps search for it but discovers two Amur hawkmoths instead, tranquilly copulating, very near the place where his father, with help, had netted a rare Peacock butterfly in 1883. (I am putting the pieces together; they are scattered in the book.) A footbridge is part of the scenery among which this lost-and-found is enacted, and it is on the Chemin du Pendu. Through the latter detail the spirit of the Decembrist Rileev, poet and duelist, haunts the experience (if not actually the place named for him), as does his more famous opponent, who haunts whole chapters (Chapter 11, for instance) and, indeed, an entire literature. The former detail leads to other footbridges: the one Nabokov crosses on the butterfly chase that issues in Colorado, and still another near the pavilion where he began his first poem, and on which he first saw and later parted so often from, his first love.

One should not make such fuss over the existence of foot-bridges in a country estate networked with paths and ghylls? Yes. But the commentary is directed at *the use in a book* made of such otherwise ordinary and ignorable structures. The themes embedded in the organized disarray of those foot-bridges, paths, and dewy ambulations are, I hope, self-assertive.

One of the most fleeting patterns involves the tunnels young Vladimir constructed from sofa and bolsters and blocks, which inform, in the summer of 1914, his sense of the "private mist" he kept merging with and emerging from as he composed his first poem. That poem is, moreover, associated with the storm its author sought refuge from in the pavilion; the pavilion rose from its surroundings "like a coagulated rainbow" and, once the storm is over another rainbow, this one in the sky, "slipped into view." Composition begins; the rainbow becomes "earthen" as the verses progress, and once the poem is finished and has a reader, only half of the rainbow remains, and that is now part of a watercolor (and parenthetical, to boot). Still, when Tamara enters in the next chapter it is at the "rainbow-windowed pavilion," and one recalls that long before any of these intense and omen-laden events occurred the author of it all has been careful to say what, in the private spectrum of his alphabet, the word for *rainbow* is.

There are other such patterns, involving most notably the association of art and love,[12] and the prefiguration of exile.[13]

---

12. Pages 73, 218, 230 and, one of the most effectively suggestive, Vladimir and Tamara, having to continue their summer affair in snowy, inhospitable St. Petersburg, meeting in "museums and movie houses" (SM, 237).

13. Pages 97, 234, and, most movingly, five-year-old Vladimir, vacationing in the Adriatic, nostalgically tracing on his pillow the "carriage road sweeping up to our Vyra house" (SM, 76). Part of a New York *Times* interview (April, 1969) reprinted in *Strong Opinions* is interesting too: see page 132 ("Yes, in part. The odd fact...").

This is no more surprising in a book whose "true purpose" is "the following of thematic designs" than it is to find in a book presided over by a contrapuntal genius a pattern of images which are themselves reticulate. The first ones are part of Nabokov's first memories: the "lateral nets of fluffy cotton cords" on his crib, the "mesh of sunshine" which greeted his emergence from the divan-tunnel, the wire mesh surrounding the new tennis court at Vyra. Two others are poignantly maternal: Madame Nabokov's veil through which he used to kiss her cheek, and whose "touch of reticulated tenderness my lips used to feel" he remembers with joy; and the "thin fabric that veiled the windowpane" of the oriel in his mother's boudoir in the large house in St. Petersburg, through which he would look out on the Morskaya. "With lips pressed against [it] I would gradually taste the cold of the glass through the gauze" (SM,89).

Nets which contain, which partly hide and obscure, which afford certain sensual pleasures—these associative values become more resonant later when they begin to form aural networks with other, more complicated activity. Lepidopterists capture their quarry with fine nets; words are a "magic veil" through which their reader may perceive a various and sparkling world, though they may be so used as to build a wall instead; the features of a lover may be fascinating but, "instead of divulging her person," Nabokov writes about Tamara, "they tended to form a brilliant veil in which I got entangled every time I tried to learn more about her" (SM,231). When he revisits Cambridge about 1939 and wanders around town in the rain, peering "at the rooks in the black network of the bare elms," he fails finally to work up for that part of his past any genuine nostalgic excitement. But when he recreates the "parks and gardens" associated with his wanderings in Europe after becoming a father the result is altogether different. The various thematic directions the series of images of reticulation

185

has suggested converge in a final focus on consciousness as Nabokov considers, while speaking of his own son, the miracle of its awakening in a child: "It occurs to me that the closest reproduction of the mind's birth obtainable is the stab of wonder that accompanies the precise moment when, gazing at a tangle of twigs and leaves, one suddenly realizes that what had seemed a natural component of that tangle is a marvelously disguised insect or bird" (SM, 298).

VI

Chapter 7, "Colette," is rivaled only by certain iridescent palimpsests in other Nabokov books for its delicate, mysterious effects. The "handful of jewels," the other emblems of exile (trains—both miniature replicas and full-sized ones; a seventy-year-old valise), of art (mirrors; the preferred pen holder "which now seems almost symbolic"), and of lepidopteral passion (Oak Eggars, Speckled Woods, Cleopatra and, yes, elusive Floss) are what excite, creating in their multiple conjunctions within the chapter (and with details in other chapters) an overtone of continuity and sadness which renders the scattered pieces of memory more than accidental or random. It is to this chapter, more than to the next one in which it appears, that the following statement applies: "There is, it would seem, in the dimensional scale of the world a kind of delicate meeting place between imagination and knowledge, a point arrived at by diminishing large things and enlarging small ones, that is intrinsically artistic" (SM, 167).

VII

To "this final edition" of *Speak, Memory* Nabokov appended an index, whose presence, he writes in the Foreword, "will annoy the vulgar but may please the discerning, if only because

Through the window of that index
  Climbs a rose

And sometimes a gentle wind *ex*
Ponto blows."

Others must judge one's discernment, but in this case I can vouch for my pleasure. I remind myself, too, lest that pleasure carry me off into transports of specific gloss, of my remarks concerning exhaustiveness at the beginning of this chapter. The resulting compromise permits me to allude only to the entries "Florence," "Honeysuckle," and "Oak Avenue": they are masterpieces of miniature intricacy, playful poignance, thematic inducement, and absolute attention, not to mention their being perfectly suited to the aforementioned notion of the intrinsically artistic. The other part of the compromise admits a more particular enlargement.

An index, like a dictionary, consists of abstracted components, and is part of a pattern of referential circularity in which its own elements may participate. It is, then, more than a convenience, more than a handy aid to paginal location. There are no entries in the index to *Speak, Memory* for "bridge" or "footbridge" (or even "pons"), and the four-entry ringaround that Nabokov *has* included may not be that "rose" to which he refers, either, but it is certainly a lovely, colorful intertwinement, and it leads frequently to that pattern of bridges on which I have already commented. It is composed of the following:

Colored hearing, 34–36. *See also* Stained glass
Stained glass, 105. *See also* Jewels *and* Pavilion
Jewels, 36, 81, 111, 143, 188, 252. *See also*
    Stained glass
Pavilion, 215–216, 230 [14]

14. To "Pavilion," page 226 should be added; for "Jewels" change 252 to 253 and add 245 (my correction and additions). As I will show, there are other pages which could be included following these four entries, but they are largely metaphorical and allusive, not "direct" references. While I am at it, to the page numbers listed after his wife's name (314) should be added 258 and 281. All instances referred to are second person, direct address.

One could begin a discussion with any one of these and be sure it would lead him eventually to the others. I would prefer, however, to use the events of Chapter 11, "First Poem," as a center, and notice how these special radii converge there.

The reconstruction will perforce be inadequate, but nevertheless let me sketch some of the early points on the journey. We encounter colored hearing first, and most briefly; the two paragraphs devoted to it conclude with the word for "rainbow," as I have mentioned in the overture to this section, but I did not point out, as the index entries do, that the last page listed for "Colored hearing" is also the first for "Jewels." Since, in fact, page 36 contains no overt references to the phenomenon of colored hearing, one infers that the description of the mass of jewelry is superimposed, so to speak, upon it. The two blend nicely, syncolorous. They are thematically compatible, too: the jewels, or rather the few remaining in the talc tin (SM, 245), will pay for expenses in London (SM, 253), and the author's unusual alphabet will sustain him in more complex and devious ways, through a long life of peregrinative exile.

But I have gotten beyond my terminal and must back up. The jewelry, "flashing tiaras and chokers and rings," seemed to Nabokov "hardly inferior in mystery and enchantment to the illumination in the city during imperial fêtes." Most of that fiery brilliance changes ownership in the winter of 1917–1918 when a "planted" servant, one Ustin, who until the incident has been rather comically presented, leads "representatives of the victorious Soviets" to their hiding place in the room where Nabokov was born (SM, 188). Foresight, as I have noted, saved some; one particular item, "a pigeon-blood ruby and diamond ring" that Madame Nabokov wore regularly, saw to it that the association with culture continued, the imperial festivities being transformed to the (parenthetical) "room, people, lights, trees in the rain—a whole period of émigré life for which that ring was to pay" (SM, 81). And as Nabokov's colored hearing merged with the colored fire of the jewels in Chapter 2, so in this second entry under "Jewels" the ring is seen as a familiar cynosure in the simultaneous domestic and literary constellation of mother reading to son in English. The jewels and the colored alphabet, then, are interwoven, so that to encounter either is to be immediately in the presence of various central themes, themselves twined together in the life of the subject: idiosyncratic and secret art, exile, persistence and perspective in severe adversity, filial love and family cohesiveness.[15]

Though much of what I have referred to comes chronologically after (some of it *long* after) Nabokov's writing of his first poem, compositionally it precedes that momentous occasion. We still have a way to go to the hub of the web, though, and the silken network we are backing and shifting on becomes even more dense before we arrive.

Mademoiselle O, in an echoic scene, reads to the Nabokov boys. The single page listed for "Stained glass" refers to this occurrence, particularly to the "harlequin pattern of colored panes inset in a whitewashed framework on either side of the veranda." The different colors of the individual panes render a number of worlds to the young auditor whose eye has wandered. And though Nabokov says his attention wandered, I don't think that's quite accurate; at the risk of an inappropriate and cheap contemporary association, I will say his mind expanded, started to compose, including with the discrete fantasies available through the panes of glass the rhythmic motions of leaves and branches, Mlle. O's expressive and totally engaged reading voice, the appearance and disappearance

---

15. The importance of the jewels extends beyond the passages that deal explicitly with them. Two representative instances: entomological exploration "from the very first . . . had a great many inter-twinkling facets" (SM, 126); on the forty-year butterfly race Nabokov sees "pretty Cordigera, a gemlike moth" (SM, 138). See as well pages 145, 152, 275, and 304.

of a butterfly, and the events in the book being read. The thought of exile is present too: there is among the colored panes a small square of "normal" glass, which "of all the windows," Nabokov says, is the one "through which in later years parched nostalgia longed to peer" (SM, 107).

The basic themes, and the central image, are focused here, but on the rest of the way to "First Poem" small details occur which act as fillips to the initial scene. Lenski's slide shows, for instance, are monuments of embarrassment to young Vladimir, "but, on the other hand, what loveliness the glass slides as such revealed when simply held between finger and thumb and raised to the light—translucent miniatures, pocket wonderlands, neat little worlds of hushed luminous hues! In later years, I rediscovered the same precise and silent beauty at the radiant bottom of a microscope's magic shaft" (SM, 166). He also likes to imagine an *al fresco* banquet where he sees "the faces of seated people sharing in the animation of light and shade beneath a moving, fabulous foliage" (SM, 171), and he sees his father's activities "through a prism of my own, which split into many enchanting colors the rather austere light my teachers glimpsed" (SM, 186).

By the time one arrives at Chapter 11, then, there is a carefully prepared context, dense with detail and thematic richness, in which the account of the poem's composition becomes almost incredibly resonant. (In fact, all but two of the pages Nabokov lists in these four entries *precede* the poem.) I have noted already the rainbow and its transformations corresponding to stages in the making of the poem. The "wine-red and bottle-green and dark-blue lozenges of stained glass" of the pavilion (yes, we are there, 215–16) complement it, as does this brief bit of inserted data: "Etymologically, 'pavilion' and 'papilio' are closely related." Further, the "cordate leaf," medieval in its—

This is perhaps a propitious place to back off. Tamara appears at the pavilion in the next chapter, deepening the resonances further. Rhetorical habit and expectation would call for a coda at this point, a summarily conclusive recapitulation which (like that phrase) would resound redundantly, satisfying the emotional requirement of the *sound* of finality, its swell and surge and sigh of repletion. It seems preferable, however, and a paradigmatic critical choice, to recede, since that motion leaves one's reader nowhere to turn except back to the book.